The Telescope in the Parlor

The Telescope in the Parlor
Essays on Life and Literature
James McConkey

PAUL DRY BOOKS
Philadelphia 2004

First Paul Dry Books Edition, 2004

Paul Dry Books, Inc.
Philadelphia, Pennsylvania
www.pauldrybooks.com

Text type: Bembo
Display type: Ellington
Composed by P. M. Gordon Associates
Designed by Adrianne Onderdonk Dudden

3 5 7 9 8 6 4 2
Printed in the United States of America

Library of Congress Cataloging-in-Publication Data

McConkey, James.
The telescope in the parlor : essays on life and literature /
by James McConkey.— 1st Paul Dry Books ed.
p.   cm.
ISBN 1-58988-020-X (alk. paper)
1. McConkey, James. 2. Novelists, American— 20th century—Biography.
3. Fiction—History and criticism. 4. Books and reading. I. Title.

PS3563.C3435Z476 2004
813'.54—dc22
2004018207

ISBN 1-58988-020-X

Contents

Preface

Deism, the religion of rationalists in the neoclassical age, presupposes a god who opted for early retirement: having created and set into motion Earth and all the other cosmic bodies, the deity had accomplished his work for all eternity. In the classical age, though, the gods were many and rarely without matters to occupy their attention. In addition to quarrelling among themselves, they interceded in the lives of humans by aiding those in their favor while injuring those who were not. Though only a minor deity, Hermes must have been among the busiest. In his role as messenger (he had other duties as well) he travelled widely, doing his best to interpret the intent of one god to another. Hermeneutics—the branch of knowledge concerned with the theories and actual practice of interpretation—owes its name to him, and so does the phrase "hermeneutical circle." That phrase is used to describe a major problem, indeed a paradox, in the interpretation of Scriptural and later texts. The circling takes this form: We must know in order to believe; and yet we must believe in order to know.

That paradoxical circling—like a dog chasing its tail—has its origin in early attempts to understand sacred texts such as the New Testament gospels. It also applies to secular texts—those that contain belief or beliefs but don't require Belief—from the simple fact that it is impossible to interpret any text as a thing-in-itself, a work separate from the knowledge we bring to it through previous readings or anything else we carry in memory. As a consequence, any assessment we might wish to make of a passage or a whole work involves a constant circling between our own assumptions and beliefs and those conveyed by the text. If we are scrupulous readers, we may find a text persuasive enough to cause us to alter, or at least to question, some of our views. Since we cannot disassociate ourselves from the material we are reading, though, a persuasive text is one that bears some congruence to our past experiences, perhaps permitting us to see what we already know in a new light. It is as difficult for us to make a wholly unbiased judgment of any text as it is for that text to bring a major change to our understanding of ourselves. Revelations are possible, but they are rare.

To what extent, if any, does this difficulty apply to the interpretations that we give to the text of our lives? The problem is different and yet similar. We interpret the present from our knowledge of the past, and yet can interpret the past only on the basis of our present knowledge. Our beliefs, whether sacred or secular in nature, have their seeds in a collective as well as a personal memory—the source also of our sense of identity. That sense of identity comes to most of us early in our development, and the attitudes and convictions that are its bulwark resist change. I am generalizing, I admit, from what I think is true of myself. Especially in my last years as a teacher, though, I began to see the same resistance in my students, though ostensibly they had come to college to learn and to know. But of course neither they nor I were made of a plastic to be shaped in the heat of anybody else's opinions. Like their instructor, they were likely to understand and accept only those ideas that did not interfere with pre-established interpretations of life and its meanings. (As for myself, to give but one example of my resistance to change, I subscribe only to periodicals that support my own beliefs or the cultural interests congenial to them.)

Despite all such evidence, it is folly to say that we are incapable of change. Looking back on my own life from my eighty-third year, I can see that I *have* changed—I suppose in an incremental way that I've barely been aware of, but on occasion quickly enough to meet a crisis, as if a little Hermes in my brain were connecting a new insight to the ones sustained over the decades. I hope I'm not deluding myself by finding that these changes reinforce rather than violate my awareness of who I am or at least want to be—that sense of identity provided to each of us by memory.

Reflections like these may seem an idiosyncratic way of introducing a volume of previously uncollected work, but they were on my mind as I made my selections for this volume (most of them written in the past decade or so) from the mass of available articles, essays, and reviews. In choosing those that most matter to me, I have discovered that I mention more than once certain writers I admire: Augustine, Proust, Virginia Woolf, E. M. Forster, and

Chekhov. Different as they are, I see in each of them spiritual affinities with the others—and with me. In referring to them, I return to specific passages in their work that for decades have moved me as expressions of subjective truths I accept. But I also return a number of times to a moment that permanently altered my perceptions. All of the essays reflect an identity that even in its alterations is resistant to change. They reflect the personal ways that life and literature alike have abetted an ongoing interpretation of human experience that can't—or won't—separate its secular and spiritual components. I am under no illusions that this slender book will alter the convictions of others— particularly of those who accept Belief without question, as well as those convinced that we have no sustaining beliefs at all—but it may be of interest to those who find some of its ways similar to ones they have followed in their own ongoing interpretations of life.

I

Three Autobiographical Essays

Personal memory provides the substance of much that I've written. In 1960, I began an exploration of the relationship of the past to the present in my own life. I've never known what to call the individual segments that make up this ongoing work; the editors of some magazines in which they have appeared define them as "memoirs," a genre I've never much liked. They are personal essays, but when they work as well as I want them to, they seem to aspire (without conscious intent) to the condition of fiction, though nothing about them is invented. (The editors of the *New Yorker,* where many of them appeared during the decades of William Shawn's leadership, saw them as "pieces," a category that conveniently refuses to distinguish fiction from nonfiction.)

Over the years, these explorations of subjective memory have been collected in books, the first, *Crossroads,* published in 1968. In 1982, those essays were combined with a later group—"The Stranger at the Crossroads"—under the title *Court of Memory*. The whole project reached its conclusion with the publication of *Stories from My Life with the Other Animals* in 1993, a date that roughly corresponds to the end of the Cold War. But to my mind, *Court of Memory*— a title I filched from Augustine's *Confessions,* the passage from which it is found serving as epigraph not only for that book but for *Stories from My Life*—is the name encompassing all three.

As Augustine realized, though, habits of the mind don't wholly vanish until the mind itself goes; and as a consequence I've found myself now and again returning to this habit, particularly in the three essays that follow. Using some of the same phrases, two of them try to describe the moment that made me the kind of writer I've become. The first essay, which provides this book with its title, contains my latest, and probably my final, attempt to do just that.

1 The Telescope in the Parlor

Ever since 1962, the year my family moved into a Greek Revival farmhouse at a country crossroads in New York's Finger Lakes region, my study has been the former parlor, a room once reserved for special occasions. Twenty years after we bought that old house and the surrounding fields and woods, I wrote an autobiographical essay or story— titled "The Laughter of Zeus," it first appeared in the *New Yorker*—which early on contains a paragraph describing my feelings on the day we began to bring our belongings into the empty rooms:

> . . . [T]he first possession I brought into the farmhouse was . . . [my] telescope, and I put it in a corner of the parlor that was to become my study. The windows of this room—the most formal in the house—are framed at the sides and top by wood that has been fluted to resemble Greek columns. After positioning the telescope on its tripod, I looked out the window at the wild-rose brambles just beyond the glass and at a field of corn whose dark-green leaves were shimmering in the August sunlight, and I was caught by the sense of a lovely strangeness that yet was familiar—a response so intense as to be astonish-

3

ing, and of the kind that perhaps comes only when the outer eye perceives what the inner one, which is blind to everything but the ideal, has all along visualized as the omphalos of the universe, as its long-sought home.

Once you find such a home, of course, it loses its ability to surprise you like that, even though the recollection remains as part of its quality. Some years ago, I replaced that telescope—a reflector with a four-inch mirror whose limited light-gathering power made it useful mainly for looking at the major spectacles of our solar system—with a Schmidt-Cassegrain refractor whose eight-inch mirror can also capture the glow of distant nebulae and separate the stars in a cluster; but as I have aged I use it less and less. It's a heavy instrument to lug out of the house into the country dark, and much of the wonder it brought me is now more accessible through memory than through its eyepiece.

But this telescope still serves me, as an instrument for remembering an even earlier moment—one that altered my life and gave me whatever voice I have as a writer. When I was younger, I said little about that moment. It was the seed from which I wrote autobiographical essays that—perhaps from my constant wish to get beyond my ego, or at least to perceive myself as a character in another writer's work—turned into interrelated stories with a first-person narrator who, with the passage of the years, was delineating his particular arc of our transitory human existence. This project was central to my writing career for three decades. Upon completing it, I began to describe more openly the moment that was—and remains—my creative seed, for it underlies my attitude to literature, politics, and life in general. Since it is essential to anything I might say about either my writing or my room, I will say it again here: That moment occurred one winter night early in the Cold War when nuclear annihilation was such a possibility that the phenomenal world became sacred, the humblest of objects (my dog's cold and moist nose; a deserted robins' nest, mounded with snow and illuminated by starlight in the bare branches of a Norway maple) interconnected with every other object, these interconnections reaching out to include the farthest star. My mind acknowledged something that every part of my body knew—something so overwhelming that if I felt anything at all, it might have been awe or fright.

Words are inadequate to describe such a moment, especially when they fall into a pattern like that: words that conform to a familiar pattern are a displacement of the actual event. But my immediate responses to that moment were its echo, the reverberations both lasting and clear. Humility was one such response. And I realized—to a degree that was painful—how fully I loved my wife and children. All the normal stuff of fiction I had depended upon—violence, the quest for dominance, the impurity of human relationships—became untenable to me, even banal. That night I became essentially a writer of my own experiences, attempting to connect the normal details of daily living to a unity I had apprehended only for an instant, and which consciousness itself has since kept from my reach. (I suppose the later moment, when I marked the parlor as my room for writing by putting the telescope in it, was my means of coping with, or adjusting to, the earlier one, by providing the cosmos with a center.) Given the enormous restrictions of my way of telling a story— no invented characters, no imagined actions to form a plot—I wouldn't recommend my approach to anybody else: mine, while it provides a spiritual insight denied to my former fiction, was imposed on me, a necessity.

The two paintings closest to the desk in my room— one an abstract watercolor by Archie Ammons which for me implies much about that poet's psyche, the other a reproduction of Rembrandt's *The Polish Rider*—are in keeping with my creative seed. Among the changing notices on my bulletin board, three items have remained constant for decades as a reminder of writers who have influenced me: a pencil sketch of E. M. Forster, a photograph of Chekhov, and a haunting paragraph from Proust's "The Return to the Present" that begins, "The fine things we shall write if we have talent enough. . . ."

The familiar artifacts on my study's walls include a resemblance to a face made by my youngest son as a child. He constructed it for me from scraps of wood and hardware he found in the woodshed, and I placed it in a corner where its eyes, round with pleasure, are appraising *The Polish Rider.* These objects are as valuable to me as the dictionaries, reference works, and volumes of poetry and prose that my overloaded bookcases contain; and so too is the view from my window. The field I look at on this July day is filled not with corn but with wide strips of oats that are still a light green, winter wheat that has already turned red, and spring-planted wheat of a darker green that seems luminescent in the sunlight. Though each fall I cut them down, the prickly strands of the wild-rose bush still rise each spring with all their old vigor, their red and pink blossoms throughout the summer months so profuse and so close to the window they seem as much a part of my room as the telescope.

2 Idyll

Toward the middle of my career as a college teacher, I had an unexpected classroom insight. Unlike my undergraduates, I had been born long before Auschwitz and Buchenwald, before the invention of the nuclear bomb, television, birth control pills, or even of Scotch tape and Bandaids; before the epidemic of mind-altering drugs, or the shocking collapse of our cities into burgeoning suburbs for the well-to-do and ghettoes for the poor. My advanced years made me, in a crucial way, younger—surely more innocent—than my students, burdened as they were almost from birth with historical knowledge that came to me in increments long after my formative years.

Like nearly all other revelations, this one—that the older we are, the younger we are—was far less original than for years I thought it to be; shortly before my retirement, I learned, in an essay by Stephen Jay Gould that relies upon Robert K. Merton's book *On the Shoulders of Giants,* that my insight is known as the Baconian Paradox, in honor of the popular formulation of it made by Francis Bacon in 1605 —even though its origin can be traced as far back as an apocryphal book of the Vulgate Bible. In my case, the insight came to me as the consequence of a student's offhand remark about sex that led me to remember a respite from military duties that I shared with my fiancée at Mammoth Cave National Park one Christmas during World War II.

Not until our fiftieth wedding anniversary—one celebrated far from home—was I able to see our holiday as something more than a self-enclosed idyll, one not only too intimate to mention but isolated by its very poignancy from our later domestic experiences. Idylls, of course, are intimate, and do demand isolation. Idylls require that their participants separate themselves from historical necessity —from a world they can hold momentarily in abeyance. The world we were keeping in check then was a world at war, with all of its bloody chaos. War commands unthinking obedience from its soldiers on military duty, but relaxes societal proscriptions, particularly those concerned with sexual conduct. Like much else that was part of Jean's and my cultural heritage—including a belief in human brotherhood that made war itself abhorrent—the moral requirement of chastity before marriage had already been subject to rapid revision. So I suppose we were naive even for the times in managing to resist a consummation of our desires—willfully innocent, perhaps, since neither of us believed that a government should have the power to legislate rules about intimate behavior, mandating an official document in advance of a permanent relationship.

Shortly before my induction into the Army in May 1943, Jean and I were engaged; we were students at the same downtown school, Cleveland College, both of us on the editorial staff of the undergraduate newspaper. For basic infantry training, I was sent to an Army camp in Georgia, as a member of a special battalion. Everybody in that battalion had just graduated from college; indeed, we had all enrolled a couple of years earlier in the Army Specialized Training Program for the same reason: to delay our military service long enough for us to get our degrees. I resented the regimentation, the training to make me an efficient killer; in body as well as mind, I felt a revulsion toward the exercises designed to teach me how to thrust a bayonet into an enemy's guts. For the first time in my life, I was unable to accomplish satisfactorily what was expected of me. Most of the others managed to succeed, and yet in every other way we seemed peers—all of us from similar cultural backgrounds, all of us members of a generation told almost from birth about the horrors of war, and whose history texts in public school, written by Charles and Mary Beard, informed their young readers that economics and not idealism had motivated our past American wars, including the Revolution itself. Now, as college graduates in a specialized program, we attended any number of classroom lectures, but none of them was designed to tell us that this war had a moral necessity lacking from the earlier ones. References to German atrocities against Jews were missing, though—like all other soldiers —the trainees in my battalion were shown graphic slides of what could happen to our penises if we engaged in casual sex without using the condoms available without cost in every day room.

From all those incredibly long days and weeks of basic training, I have but one sharp memory, all of its details made vivid by the happiness I felt. On an extended night-time march, I broke step to plant one foot firmly on a ribbon of steel at a railroad crossing near a darkened Georgia hamlet, thinking that to do so connected me through a variety of switches and tracks to the passenger depot in East Cleveland, Ohio, a block or two from the house where my beloved lay sleeping.

Upon the completion of basic training, nearly all the soldiers in my battalion were sent back to college, to learn foreign languages and advanced skills in mathematics; a handful of us, dropped from the program as inept soldiers, were assigned as infantry privates to a division preparing for combat at a base in southern Kentucky, near the Tennessee border. Long before Christmas, I reserved a room for Jean at the base guest house for the holiday period, since the brevity of my pass would prevent me from returning to Cleveland. Travel was chiefly by train in those days, and the majority of the rolling stock of the railroads had been requisitioned for military use; train service for civilians was erratic and largely limited to antique passenger cars with straw seats and tulip-shaped overhead lamp brackets. Jean's 425-mile journey from Cleveland took eighteen hours, including a stopover in Cincinnati; the train from Cincinnati to Clarksville, Tennessee, was so crowded that she and many others sat on their suitcases, which wouldn't have been so difficult, she told me, if she and the others in the aisles hadn't had to rise and push aside their suitcases so often, to let the vendors of apples and soft drinks pass. She arrived the night preceding Christmas Eve, tired and smudged with soot but happy that we would be together.

Only the kind intercession of a USO volunteer kept Jean from returning to Cleveland the next evening. Her reservation at the guest house was abruptly cancelled late in the afternoon of her first full day on the base, apparently to accommodate a last-moment request by officers for their wives or friends; the few hotels and rooming houses in the nearby towns had long since been booked to capacity. I packed my weekend bag on the unlikely chance that something would turn up; harried as she was, the woman at the USO housing desk in Clarksville took a particular interest in our predicament, intensified as it was by our wish for separate rooms, and was able to secure reservations for us at the hotel within Mammoth Cave National Park, only ninety miles away. Darkness had long since fallen, and we had to rush to the station to catch the northbound train—the same one that Jean would have taken by herself, if we'd not found a place to stay. Shortly before midnight on Christmas Eve, the train stopped, just for us—for an infantry private and his fiancée!—at a little trackside sign marked "Cave City."

The helpfulness of nearly everybody we met, from the USO volunteer onward, contributed to the specialness of our brief holiday. The conductor held up the train in the apparent emptiness of the Kentucky countryside long enough to point out a path through the weeds that would take us across a road to a light that marked a telephone booth, where we could call a taxi. I called the after-hours number of the taxi company; the driver's wife, who answered the phone, said the family had just begun to open their Christmas presents, so we'd have to be patient. Less than ten minutes later, though, the taxi arrived: the driver thought the weather (we hadn't even noticed that a cold drizzle had started to fall) too miserable to leave us waiting. The hotel was a two-story frame building maybe ten minutes away; a large evergreen near the entrance glowed with colored lights. The driver carried Jean's bag into the lobby. He refused a tip, wishing us and the clerk at the registration desk—a boy of about fifteen—a merry Christmas. In an alcove off the lobby, a log fire was burning in a stone hearth; the alcove was just large enough for a couple of upholstered chairs and a small table with a checkerboard. A pair of white-framed and many-paned glass doors separated the lobby from the much larger dining room—empty of guests at this hour of course, but with another Christmas tree that lit up a series of linen-covered tables, each decorated with its own miniature tree.

Breakfast would be waiting for us in that dining room, the clerk said; he'd have to wake us quite early, in order for us to take the daylong Christmas trip led by a park ranger through the cave. For servicemen, the guided tour was free. Since Mammoth Cave itself was the only reason for the hotel's existence, he took it for granted that we would go: as I remember, he gave us our tickets after we'd signed the registration book. He led us down a long corridor to our first-floor rooms. It turned out that they were connected, as was the case throughout the hotel, by a bathroom serving both rooms. The clerk said he could lock the deadbolt of one of the bathroom doors if we wished him to, though it meant that one of us would have to use the lavatory at the far end of the hall. How strange it now seems that both of us were embarrassed, and that the adolescent clerk himself—no doubt a high school student brought in as a holiday substitute—was blushing!

Jean and I decided the deadbolt lock wasn't necessary. On that first night, we slept in our separate rooms, but with both bathroom doors open. I woke on occasion to hear laughter and music from a party down the hall, or the sound of the rain at the window, and imagined I could hear Jean stirring in her sleep.

At breakfast, the guests included those partying the night before, two WAC officers and their male civilian companions. It was still raining—as it did for most of our stay—but it didn't matter, since we and the other guests spent the daylight hours of Christmas Day underground, with a box lunch provided for us on picnic tables in a vast cavern. We had crossed three counties, the ranger said as we came to the surface by a country road where a bus was waiting to transport us back to the hotel. My recollection of our exploration of underground spectacles is far less distinct than are my memories of sitting across the table from Jean that night in the hotel restaurant, with its white linen, courteous attendants bearing platters of holiday food, and its Christmas tree, whose colored lights were reflected in her eyes; afterwards, of sitting opposite her again, this time in the lobby alcove's upholstered chairs, where we played checkers before the log fire; and finally of lying next to her on her bed or mine (she in her nightgown and I in my khaki Army shorts) where we talked long into the night about whatever came into our minds. We argued about which one of us was better at checkers; we reminisced about our first meeting (as a janitorial assistant at the college, I had been assigned an early morning task of dusting the tops of the lockers in the women's lavatory area: embarrassed that a young woman had entered who might or might not see me crouched above her on the lockers, I called out, "Don't mind me: I'm just working my way through college"); and we imagined what we might do after the war ended. We could, for example, move to some town with lovely old houses set far back from the tree-lined streets, a town in which we would raise a family while editing together the weekly newspaper.

Jean said she needed to warn me about one thing, after we'd married and moved to that little town—since childhood, she'd twisted about a lot in bed. "Like this," she said, rolling over and over so rapidly that even I became dizzy, from laughing as well as from watching her whirl. "But that's because you've been sleeping alone," I said, pulling her close. She pretended to roll again, but lay quietly, her head resting on my shoulder. (The two couples down the hall had resumed their riotous partying and whatever else it led to; only momentarily was our own resolute chastity in serious doubt.) I woke in the morning, smelling the sweetness of Jean's hair on the pillow we shared.

We had arranged with the taxi driver to pick us up at nightfall the day after Christmas for the longer ride to Bowling Green, where Jean would board the train taking her home and I the one returning me to Clarksville. We dawdled over meals, and walked along the gravel paths of the hotel grounds, despite the rain; and we let the warmth of the log fire dry the dampness from our clothes while we played more aimless games of checkers. We didn't speak much; just to hold hands while looking into the other's eyes brought us close to the tears of imminent loss. But when the taxi driver asked us if we had enjoyed our stay, we smiled and said words like Yes, very much—words which, however true, couldn't begin to indicate how we truly felt. In Bowling Green, the train station was packed with travellers heading north and south. Jean's train arrived first. Swept aboard in the jostling army of passengers eager for a seat, she made her way down an aisle already crowded with standees; sometimes from the platform I could see only the tip of the jaunty feather of her hat. My sense of loss turned into anguish at the thought that she probably wouldn't find a seat; I prayed that she would. I remember nothing about my own train ride back to Clarksville.

About four months later—on May 6, 1944—we were married, during the furlough granted all members of my division preceding our departure for Europe.

To celebrate our fiftieth anniversary, Jean and I spent a couple of weeks in New Zealand. We went there for a number of reasons. We wanted to go somewhere by ourselves, partly to prevent the fuss our three sons and extended family members would have made if we had stayed home; since childhood, Jean had dreamed of visiting those far-away islands; and New Zealand, according to the guidebooks, was a reasonably prosperous and peaceful democracy that had not despoiled the landscapes—glacier-topped mountains, rainswept fjords, green valleys filled with sheep, rugged coasts with pristine beaches—that made it one of the most beautiful places in the world.

Though graffiti were beginning to appear on city walls, we felt as if we had been transported back in time to the idealized America of our childhood, if not earlier than that. (In one town, we watched a group of adolescents dismount from their bicycles long enough to pick up some litter in the street and toss it into a nearby basket.) The kindness bestowed upon us was like that given long ago by a USO volunteer, a train conductor, and a taxi driver; but then it had much to do with the Christmas season, and with what had to be obvious to anybody who saw us—we were young and in love, and I was in uniform. Now, of course, almost everybody was much younger than we, and maybe we reminded others of their grandparents; as for the people our own age whom we met, their generosity might have come from the fact that I had been an American soldier in a distant war. "We're still grateful to you Yanks, for saving us from the Japs," a silver-haired pharmacist told me; for, by the time of Pearl Harbor, the majority of New Zealand's own troops were fighting with the British in Europe. "Yip, we know we're a kindly people," a mechanic who had come to rescue us from a car breakdown told Jean with disarming frankness. "That's because there's still so few of us in a free and beautiful land." The low population density of that land—

less than three-and-a-half million people in a pair of islands a bit larger than the Great Britain from which the
ancestors of almost everybody not a Maori had come—
has something to do with its remoteness from the West;
the consideration its people give to strangers may also be
a consequence of their knowledge that loneliness is
bonded to their good luck.

Loneliness has far more than an alliterative connection
with love as well as luck. Loneliness—that response to a
separation either real or portended—is what we feel most
strongly during the first and painful stirrings of adolescent
love; it is what we would assuage in marriage. But the
luckier and longer the marriage, the greater the awareness
of the inevitable separation. On the morning of our last
day in New Zealand, I was having thoughts—if feelings
can be called thoughts—of this kind. We had checked out
of our hotel in Queenstown, a resort on the South Island
nestled between the mountains and a lake. While waiting
for the local flight that would take us to the international
airport at Christchurch, we took a stroll in Queenstown
Gardens, where the late roses were still in full bloom; at
home, our buds would just be opening. That last day was
also the anniversary day of our wedding. Just before the
ceremony, the minister, who disapproved of wartime mar-
riages, said he supposed his advice that we postpone ours
had come too late to do any good. During the ritual itself,
his words and our responses echoed in the vast emptiness
of a vaulted auditorium: only members of our immediate
families were in attendance. We were still standing at the
altar, for I had just finished kissing the bride, when a girl

of six or seven—much as all Italians do in their cathedrals, this American child was taking a shortcut home through the church—looked at the sudden paleness on my face and asked me if I wanted a glass of water. But the expectations and anxieties of a previously chaste couple on their wedding day, as well as the gratified release that follows, are so extraordinary that they provide few if any of the later associations so necessary to the reverberations of memory; it was Christmas at Mammoth Cave that I was now remembering, as if that idyll had been merely a prelude, a foreshadowing of what was yet to come. The association was a quick and simple one: having crossed through the gardens, we were standing on the lake shore, uncertain of where to go next. We sat on a rock. I grasped Jean's hand, we looked into each other's eyes, and for a moment we were sitting before the hearth in the alcove of a friendly old hotel, pretending to be engrossed in checkers while waiting for the taxi we didn't want to come. Is it sentimental to acknowledge that one's own marriage, whatever its problems, has been the idyll, all along? I don't think so, given the anguish that idylls bring. Jean, while not privy to the particular associations that had taken her with me so far back in time, still knew the reason for my sudden grief.

Mammoth Cave Hotel, I've heard, was long ago replaced by a brick motel with all the modern conveniences: it has vanished from Earth, along with our innocence. About that innocence, I'm of two minds, knowing that innocence is relative to its time and often is the result of moral blindness, while also believing that the trust of young lovers in each other's integrity—despite (or because of) the vagaries, the hypocrisies, and the growing problems of the world beyond them—is essential to whatever happiness they conceivably will find. "I am older, hence I am younger" is a paradox that allows us some defiance against a relentless forward chronology; still, the children who are our elders have a vulnerable innocence of their own that time itself will undo. Aphorisms cling to us like barnacles as we age.

On our way home, having crossed the International Date Line before reaching our stopover in Tahiti, Jean and I were able to celebrate our fiftieth anniversary for a second consecutive day. This may not have been a logical paradox, but it was an unexpected delight to toast each other with champagne from a hotel balcony that evening while watching the volcanic mass of a neighboring island turn into a scattering of mysterious lights across the darkening tropical sea.

3   Happy Trails to All

Aided by our children, Jean and I made a trail through our woods a long time ago. It begins in a long alley between two rows of black walnuts, crabapples, and other shrubby trees on our land, and crosses a seasonal creek (originally we bridged it with boards spiked to railroad ties, but when that washed away we installed a large culvert) to make an erratic loop through the woods, with a spur leading to a glen near a ravine. A now-abandoned tree house is nearby. With the help of our youngest son and my namesake, Jim, I built that little dwelling in the trees almost thirty years ago, about six years after we finished the trail. We erected it between two mature beeches on the slope of the ravine —trees taller than most, for, unlike the other hardwoods, the beeches were never considered valuable enough to harvest. A larger creek flows over rocks sixty-five or seventy feet below it.

The tree house's interior is big enough to hold a couch for sleeping, folding chairs, and a bookcase. It has a pair of windows, one full-sized with a screen as well as glass, and two doors—one for entrance, the other for access to a railed porch high above the ravine. We built it as sturdily as we could, using redwood siding bought at a bargain price, the pressure-treated floor studs supported by beams a previous owner of our old farmhouse had stored in one of the barns—wood so hard that I had to drill holes not only for lag bolts but for spikes. Every evening, we calculated the length of the boards we would need the next day, for we cut the wood with a power saw at home, transporting it the following afternoon the half-mile into the woods in a cart attached to a garden tractor.

The house itself has lasted pretty well over the decades, though the siding has been scratched at and nibbled by squirrels trying to gain entrance. The weakest part is the green fiberglass roof, chosen for its light weight and the way it merges with the color of the leaves; years ago (but long after Jim had left home), I had to repair the damage to it made by a falling bough. I didn't want the tree house to disintegrate, for my wife and I still visited it for picnic lunches and occasionally, on a warm summer night, we slept there. Ultimately, in a violent wind storm, the upper part of one of the trees, a section maybe twenty feet in length, was ripped off in such a way that the tree house beneath it wasn't damaged. Now that the house was so fully exposed, I could see that it was at a slight tilt. In building it, we had used a level to make sure that the supporting beams were precisely horizontal. They now slanted down, toward the beech that had lost its canopy, and the strain caused by the change had splintered the beams where they were attached by lag bolts to that tree, making the tree house too hazardous to enter. I've heard it said that the trunk of a tree may grow thicker, but that its height upward is only achieved at the top: that is to say, the bole at any point remains constant, the lowest branches not growing up with the bole but simply dying and falling off as the upper canopy prevents light from reaching their leaves. And it is true enough that the barbed wire attached a century ago to the trees that separate the woods from the nearby field has not grown upward, though it has become firmly embedded within the widening trunks.

Still, I found it difficult to accept that trees grow upward only that way, probably because unconsciously I've always assumed a likeness between my body and other living things and I knew that *my* trunk had grown throughout my younger years, my upper limbs rising. Could it be that higher up, the boles of trees don't remain constant at any given point, and that the trunk of one of these beeches had grown at a faster rate? Either that had happened, or the woody cells beneath the bark of the other tree, maybe older and obviously less supple than its mate, had become compressed by the weight of the now-toppled upper section.

When I saw the damage for the first time, a couple of analogies occurred to me that favored the latter view. Surprisingly enough, my body also provided the initial one. Having achieved my full height and then maintaining it for some decades, I began to shrink as I neared my seventieth birthday. According to the pencil markings on the kitchen doorframe that show my height against the various heights of our three sons as they reached and then far exceeded that mark, I've lost an inch and a half, even though I have to buy shoes two sizes larger than I once did. The second analogy, which stems from the first, came from an observation that Jim recounted to my wife and me. As a college upperclassman, he had participated in an ongoing research project led by a Cornell dendrochronologist to date the age of old timbers in the Mediterranean region. Jim had climbed high on a ladder in Santa Sophia at Istanbul to drill out a tiny cylinder of wood from one of the beams. The interior of that vast building gives the illusion of weightlessness, the golden dome above almost seeming to float above the windows that rim it. Actually, four arches support that dome, one at each corner of the square area beneath it. In entering the building, Jim had noticed that the bases of the columns under the arches had thickened: over the centuries the marble and porphyry of those pillars had been so compressed by the weight above that the stone was spreading out on the floor like wax.

Like anybody else's memory, mine is always at work, making analogies for the sake of understanding; but I suppose to another I would seem a fine example of vainglory for comparing myself to Santa Sophia while looking at that doomed little dwelling in the trees. Unlike Santa Sophia, though, that tree house was embedded in my life. As I was aware when Jim and I first chose that pair of beeches for its location, it was but yards away from the glen where he had hidden in the grass with Jean and me. In 1962, when we bought our already old farmhouse, we had lacked the funds to purchase much of the land that had always been part of the property; but by 1966 we managed, through luck and a new mortgage, to gain the remaining fields and woods. One spring afternoon, Jean and I decided to mark the route for the trail in our new woods before the concealing leaves came out. Jim—he was Jimmy then—came along, for he was still too young for the first grade. We left a note on the front door for his two older brothers to read after the school bus dropped them off that told them they could find us by following the strips of red cloth we would be attaching to the saplings and tree branches in the woods. Something as elusive as a transitory present feeling has often caused me over the years to remember that brief interval after Jimmy and Jean and I first heard the distant cries of the older boys, and then the sound of the twigs crackling under their feet as they neared the nest in the tall grass where we sat. How does one explain the extraordinary happiness it brought to Jean and me and obviously to Jimmy, whose eyes were shining? I've thought of it as a moment that confirmed our separate identities as well as the identity of our family; as a confirmation by the earth; as a fulfillment. But the three of us in the grass, having left clues to our location, were, as I have said, simply waiting. It has taken the passage of many years for me to realize that the qualities I have ascribed to that interval were, and are, anticipatory.

For that matter, most of the other values I ascribe to the tree house (which in my mind always has commemorated that moment in the tall grass nearby) also are anticipatory. They come far less from the uses to which we put it over the decades than from the evening hours that

Jimmy and I spent drawing diagrams of its dimensions, buying or finding suitable materials (discarded storm windows, for example), and slowly watching the house materialize while we hammered, meanwhile imagining how it would feel to spend a night in the trees or to sit on a chair on the porch, looking down on our domain of creek, ravine, and glen. Even when the structure was completed, we had a final problem to solve, for in Jimmy's eyes it was a little castle in the trees and like any castle required security while its inhabitants slept or were away—some equivalent, that is, to a moat and drawbridge. The dilemma seemed beyond resolution until it occurred to me upon awakening one morning that the answer lay in the long extension ladder we had used to construct the building. By reversing the ladder—that is, by attaching the wider base section far up the trunk—we could use the rope on the extension section to raise or lower it to the ground. Once he was inside the tree house, Jimmy could raise the extension, if he wished to; when he was away, he could lift it from the ground, throwing the rope safely out of sight on the little platform we had built before the front door. To retrieve the rope, we could find or fashion a fifteen-foot-pole with a crook on its end—a pole he could hide in the underbrush while he was away. Having solved the final problem, we quickly furnished the interior; Jimmy felt it secure enough to fill a shelf with his favorite books.

As I've said, I thought of my body and then of Santa Sophia when I first saw that the tree house had tilted.

Santa Sophia (*Hagia Sophia,* or Holy Wisdom, in Greek) was built by the Emperor Justinian to replace a previous Christian basilica destroyed by fire, and though its dome collapsed in 558 as a consequence of earthquakes, it was rebuilt in its present form in 563. Whatever the pressure on its columns, and despite numerous earthquakes and political turmoil, it has survived as a supreme example of Byzantine architecture. Following the Turkish conquest of Constantinople—now Istanbul—in 1453, Santa Sophia was transformed from a basilica to a mosque. Its mosaics were covered with plaster, and four minarets were erected outside. (The original building, with the added minarets, became the model for mosques built everywhere else.) Presently it serves only a secular purpose, as a museum, with the mostly empty building itself the major attraction.

About forty-five years ago, as a newly appointed assistant professor at Cornell, I was assigned to teach a freshman English course that included among its texts Herbert J. Muller's *The Uses of the Past.* In that book, Santa Sophia serves as archetype for all the ironies to be found in human history. My son Jim was not yet born when my students and I were trying to speak intelligently about the ironies of history on Tuesday, Thursday, and Saturday mornings at 8 A.M.; but years later, when Jim, now a Cornell student himself, was at the top of an extension ladder far taller than the one in our woods, he observed a contemporary irony taking place under the echoing dome of that austere but once-sacred edifice. A scene for a movie was being filmed; portable lights illuminated a young, scantily dressed actress and the lion whose leash she was holding. By the time Jim had climbed down, the scene had been completed, the lion coerced by its trainer back into a cage. The name of the film, the director told him, would be *Lion Man 2*. When Jim said he hadn't seen its predecessor, the director said there wasn't one, but that the film could be marketed more successfully if it was perceived as a sequel.

Irony comes from detachment, an emotional remove I didn't have when I climbed the tree-house ladder for the last time. Opening the door, I could see Jim's old books, the propane lantern hanging from its hook, the fire extinguisher I had attached to the wall for an unexpected emergency, the couch big enough to serve as a bed, the chairs waiting to be sat upon. Everything was as it had been, but nothing could be salvaged; the splintered beams beneath the floor might break under my weight. The single item I could save was the ladder, which I brought home. Having never seen Santa Sophia, Jean and I might welcome the unlikely chance; but for several years I refused to go near the tree house, leaning as it does between a still-healthy tree and another whose top has been blasted off.

Like memory itself, which constructs images from the past, imagination depends on what is not presently before us, which suggests the intimate relationship between these two faculties. For Proust, the unwilled and thus wholly unexpected memory of an event is superior to the event itself, for memory, transfigured by imagination, can transcend time in these involuntary returns to the past. In their return, they reveal the eternal essence of things, bringing us the happiness that, however transitory, justifies and gives value to our normally mundane existence. He uses thousands upon thousands of words in volume after volume to communicate to himself and to us what is really beyond words to express, sending off in the process of writing his lovely and rhythmic sentences so many phosphorescent bullets, each gracefully arcing tracer illuminating (if it doesn't pierce) the human psyche, that I am ready to believe him when, nearing the end, he pulls the strands of his long narrative together by willing his narrator to reexperience a number of those unwilled moments that are beyond time. They explode in succession like fireworks, the fading emotions of one psychic display replaced by the next.

And yet, increasingly as I have aged (and I am now almost three decades older than was Proust when he died, his monumental merger of life and art not quite revised to his satisfaction), my unwilled memories are of moments or episodes that were—like that interval in which the three of us were nestled in the grass—anticipatory in nature. As such, they cannot be divorced from time, and so would seem distinct from, if not opposed to, the values of Proust's involuntary memory. Without the use of all those supporting elements that art uses to suspend disbelief, it is difficult for me—not a fictive presence but a human whose life journey remains exploratory, even now—to make plausible the single moment in my life that truly struck me as beyond time, and hence beyond words. It occurred one winter night early in the Cold War when nuclear annihilation was such a possibility that the phenomenal world became sacred, the smallest object (a deserted robins' nest mounded with snow and illuminated by starlight in the bare branches of a backyard Norway maple) interconnected with every other object. But it had nothing to do with any earlier experience I was aware of, so it was not a memory transformed by imagination, and it brought no happiness then, nor does it now as I attempt to describe it. It was simply an acknowledgment by my mind of something felt in every part of my body, something so overwhelming that if I felt anything at all, it might have been awe or fright; but my words now only falsify that experience. It changed my life and gave me a voice as a writer, but I can't relive it. Because of my reliance on personal memory, I have been called a memoirist, though I don't consider myself one, at least in the conventional sense; for all I've ever wanted to do was to connect the ever-changing details of daily living to a lost but hardly paradisiacal moment that transcended time.

What I can and do relive without conscious volition are various seemingly trivial instances, some of them occurring more than a half century ago, remembered not because of what imagination today brings to them, but for what it brought to the actual experience. The heightened effect of all such experiences lies in a qualitative and wholly subjective possibility. It may be a contradiction of the normal definition of the term to say it, and perhaps I shouldn't generalize from personal experience; nevertheless, I think that imagination, especially when we are young, constructs emotions in advance of mental images—

or at least refuses to envision them as more than a generalized mental pattern until it finds a specific image from the material world that is worthy of its emotional coloration and possible transformation.

For the past decade, for example, I have been remembering—in an almost obsessive way, but without the irritation that accompanies the unwanted recall of a commercial slogan or an insipid tune—two incidents saved from oblivion by the happiness of an elusive promise. Both of them are from my high school years in the Ohio village of Olmsted Falls—where, because my parents were divorced and unable to provide for me, I was living with an aunt (my mother's sister) and uncle—and both involve walking. In the first, I am walking with a friend down an unfamiliar country road, one devoid of traffic. We must have been walking for miles, for night has come and a full moon is rising. We pass through the shadows of roadside trees; distant dogs are barking, and the windows of the scattered farmhouses are occasionally lit, though I see no inhabitants within. The night is pleasantly cool. This is all I remember of that journey. I don't even remember who my companion is. I think he and I had been given free tickets to the major-league baseball game that afternoon (the games were always played in the daylight hours then, at League Park in a crowded residential area on Cleveland's east side), and I believe that afterwards we took a streetcar to the end of its line, walking from there; but none of the factual details—including who won the game —have remained with me, only the happiness of walking through the moonlit night toward a goal. But what could that goal have possibly been? The ostensible destination may have been a Boy Scout camp, though I was never a Scout, since I have the vague recollection of a series of barracks-like buildings, all of them dark. I think we may have come across our physics teacher, who also coached the baseball team for which I was an outfielder, sitting on the ground and smoking a cigar. He may even have offered each of us a puff, making us queasy, but here I am beginning to embroider, for the memory is vanishing; and certainly no such symbolic invitation into adulthood has anything to do with the value of the memory itself.

In the second unwilled return to that period, anticipatory images have begun to form, but their vagueness is part of their appeal. This second walk, also at night, was a much shorter one, and the moon (if it was up) was hidden, along with much else, by a heavy fog. I am alone, on my way home from some unremembered event at the high school, and I am passing beneath the translucent gray umbrella of one street light after another, the street light immediately ahead only a dim glow. For more than a year, I have been a stringer for the Cleveland *Press.* Apparently I have the talent to write little feature stories about my community that are of interest to readers elsewhere. Nearly all of my stories are printed in the newspaper, sometimes even on the front page, and some are reprinted elsewhere (and on occasion come back to me, however distorted, in such national periodicals for high school students as the *American Observer*). Because of the publicity I've brought to the village, some of its residents want me to enter their professions upon my graduation. One of them is the head of the Cleveland office of a major advertising agency who has interviewed me while we sit on opposite sides of an imposing desk, the polish of its dark surface gleaming in a band of sunlight. Another is the chief meteorologist in the region, whose office is high in a tower at the nearby Cleveland airport. He says that if I pass the Civil Service exam, which will give me no trouble, I can join him. It appeals to me, this thought of working at his side, writing reports maybe, and looking at white clouds in the blue sky or the stars at night as one airplane or another takes off or descends. Or I might enter the field of journalism: wouldn't the *Press* or some other newspaper be willing to employ me? Like the dim glow through the fog of the next marker on my homeward journey, each of these choices is such a romantic possibility that I am both free and heady with elation.

In his *Confessions,* Saint Augustine poses a famous question: "What, then, is time? If nobody asks me, I know; if I want to explain it to him who asks, I don't know." Part of the problem is that the present in which we live is, as William James and others have said, "specious," for its arrival brings its disappearance. The seeming reality of any instant comes from past and future. Memory gives coherence—the weight of meaning—to the ever-passing present by relating it to the past; and, from its knowledge of that past, memory also lets us anticipate the future. I find it intriguing in this regard that neuroscientists go against common wisdom by declaring that we have memories of the possible future as well as of the past.

I may be in my eightieth year, but I'm still trying to explore and understand my own psyche. It almost scares me to say it, but I consider my life so lucky that I feel blessed. I always enjoyed the work that supported my growing family: the first paycheck I received gave me a kind of puritanical guilt, as payment for fun. I love and respect my sons, their characters as well as their achievements over the odds (including the genetic ones) that face us all. I think that the attachment between Jean and me has deepened over the fifty-six years of our life together into the kind of bond that marriage partners can only promise each other at the altar. Despite the concluding words of the chorus in Sophocles' *Oedipus the King* (less accurate than some though it may be, the translation that always comes first to my mind is "Call no man happy until he carries his happiness down to the grave in peace"), I told myself a number of years ago that Jean and I had won. So recently that I had already commenced this account, I came into the kitchen for a fresh cup of coffee and found her in tears. When I asked the reason, she said that she had just been listening—the little kitchen radio, tuned to a National Public Radio station, was still on, playing at low volume a familiar melody—to Garrison Keillor's *The Writer's Almanac*. As his poem for the day, he had recited that well-known sonnet by Shakespeare linking love to the ever-growing awareness of mortality—to the knowledge that life, like a fire, ultimately consumes itself. "This thou perceiv'st, which makes thy love more strong," the concluding couplet has the lover tell his beloved, "To love that well which thou must leave ere long."

Later that day, she said to me, "But we *have* won, haven't we?" It was more a brave affirmation than a question.

Maybe only those who are embittered, who feel cheated by life, fear death. Neither Jean nor I fear the extinguishing of our own lives: but will the one who survives the nullification of the other's consciousness be strengthened enough by the past to feel himself or herself still a victor?

By winning, you obviously lose an enormous amount; but only a fool can complain.

In one of the clichés of academic jargon, a newly appointed assistant professor is said to be "on the ladder," if only on the lowest rung. If all goes well, he or she will be tenured and on the way upward through the ranks to full professor, and maybe ultimately even to a chaired professorship. Metaphors of ascension through time also exist in the other professions, even as, in regard to the soul, they do in the metaphysics of Christianity and other religions. Goals are the expectancies above and beyond us. The psyche—the human soul—feeds on anticipation, for the soul, I have come to believe, is either a desire or nothing at all. If it is a desire, then it too would lose by winning, of course. But as we age, the wondrous expectancies once found in the vastness of the future gradually transform into those that exist in the past. To provide it with nourishment and pleasure, maybe my own soul has led me—I see no other motive for such unwilled returns—to relive those occasions of walking (in the moonlight or through the fog) when anticipation was strong within me, however inchoate or unspecified the desire.

In the conventional image, a hoary Father Time holds a
scythe in one hand and an hourglass in the other. As em-
blem of our fate, he is something of an automaton, a
clockwork figure; when the last grain of sand leaves the
upper globe to fall through the tiny aperture of the present moment into the lower globe, he will be activated to
swing the scythe. Memory is something quite different
and maybe requires the hourglass to be turned upside
down, with the past now representing its potentiality.
Memory can't be born until enough grains of sand have
fallen into its globe to form some rudimentary pattern of
likenesses or analogies, either as feelings or images. No
doubt a desire for succor from physical wants or spiritual
needs accompanies memories so early in us they leave no
later trace. In this sense if in no other, anticipation is born
with memory itself, and so has its source in the past.

Swann's Way was once my bedtime reading; as a young
man, I would commence it any number of times, falling
asleep long before the child Marcel did. I'm glad that I
didn't finishing my reading of the entirety of Proust's vast
work until I had completed much of my own writing, for
far too many of the personal discoveries that stimulated
me onward already existed in the later volumes of *Remem-
brance of Things Past*. As it nears the end, the first-person
narrator says, "We can only imagine what is absent," something obviously true, and a little later he makes the famous
judgment that "the true paradises are the paradises that we
have lost," a subjective truth that has my agreement. The
novel here is undergoing the magical process whereby
Marcel, a quasi-autobiographical character at best, is being
transformed into the Proust who, at the end, ostensibly

will begin writing all the volumes we have just read—a circling in time chronicling a search for a timeless essence that, even if briefly found, now can endlessly recur. Anticipation motivates the book—Proust's own desire, over the many years of its composition, to defeat mortality through art—and it's hardly surprising that his extraordinary achievement would seem to him, as he was dying, as still not quite complete.

Most of us seek fulfillment in life alone, not in its fusion with art. However fortunate our lives, most of us will never know Proust's degree of completion; and since we're still alive at twenty or forty or eighty, we're by definition still incomplete. Fate, being anything but capricious, will intervene; maybe we establish new goals in part to thwart it.

One such goal is the seed of this essay, my words to be completed in its telling.

About five years ago, the farmland adjoining ours was divided into a series of strips to be auctioned off to the highest bidders—a common enough practice when a township has no control over land use. Jean and I have come to think of ourselves as guardians rather than proprietors of our fields and woods; and it makes no practical sense for a couple our age, especially a couple not engaged in farming, to buy fifty or more additional acres. To maintain the pastoral setting we love, though, we did just that.

The new land begins just beyond the tree house and extends into the woods on both sides of the creek at the bottom of the ravine; it includes the remains of what may have been a dam as well as an undulating mound or earthwork more than a quarter of a mile long with dug holes at each end that over the years gradually have been filling in. From the porch of the tree house, I once could see some of these archeological remains. Had the Iroquois erected a palisade on the earthwork, to protect a now-vanished village? Two summers ago, I persuaded an archeologist who was excavating the nearby site of a known Indian village to look at these remains; their meaning was beyond her province, and she suggested that they might be prehistoric. Since it was their mystery that appealed to me, I didn't mind her inability to solve it.

At any rate, on my seventy-ninth birthday in early September, Jean asked me what I would like to do to celebrate the day. Without thinking, I responded in a way that surprised both of us. I said that what I would most like to do was once again to take strips of cloth into the woods, this time to mark a continuation of the spur trail that now ended at the tree house. What I had in mind was to clear a trail that led more or less along the edge of the ravine, past the remains of the dam (if that indeed was what it was) and maybe a third of a mile beyond it—whatever distance it took for the land to slope down to the creek below. Her ready agreement made me happy enough to be willing to pass that abandoned tree house, full of old possessions but without a ladder even to see them; and so we spent the day getting scratched in the raspberry and multiflora rose brambles as we surveyed, and then marked, the most feasible route.

In the following weeks and months, as the weather and our inclination permitted, we used a chain saw and pruning shears to extend the trail to the creek. We built two small bridges over muddy places where in spring and fall the rivulets run. It's been strenuous but playful work— maybe the American equivalent of constructing an English folly. I had thought only Jean and I enjoyed our woods, and so was twice surprised by bearded men of roughly my age who knocked at the door. Each of them lived at least a mile away; each had come to compliment us on the attractiveness of the trail, especially of its bridges, and to offer his help if we wished to continue it onward. I imagine that both have been retired from their occupations for a long time and that hunting is now their major interest; still, the thought of making trails obviously appealed to the child in each of them.

I was flattered by their praise, and said I'd phone them if we needed help. On the creek bank opposite the present terminus of the trail, an opening in the woods is the only indication that an earlier path might have gone that way. If so, the route (after skirting the largest and most beautiful bed of myrtle I've ever seen in the wild) would have headed back in the general direction of the earthwork that humans long ago made, for reasons known only to them. The goal I have in mind is to construct a trail that leads to the earthwork, on the opposite side of the ravine from the tree house, which may have collapsed by the time we get there. It will represent, I suppose, that kind of circling in time available to us, one that returns the ever-moving present to a past that existed long before we were born.

We're in no hurry to get there.

II

Eight Essays about Literature

Both the first and last essays in this section are about rereading—the first of a novel from my adolescence and the other of poetry I initially read in my middle years. The first serves as a bridge between this section and the previous one; for though the subject is literature, the essay is clearly autobiographical. And yet, to varying degrees, all of the essays in this section are personal, since I can't separate the act of reading from the countless and varied acts of living.

In preparing *Court of Memory* for book publication, I felt the need of a brief preface to say something about that star-filled winter night early in the Cold War mentioned in the previous section, for it explained the reason that I had turned from fiction to autobiographical essays of a particular nature. None of the essays ever mentions that moment, though, maybe out of my fear that repetition of it would either destroy its memory or turn it into the kind of rhetoric that is based on illusion and lies. Upon the completion of the last volume of my project in 1993, I found myself referring to that moment more openly, as is the case in the title essay and in "Happy Trails to All." In writing the latter, I thought it might be my last autobiographical essay and wanted it to stand as a testimonial (one requiring that moment) to a nearly-completed life.

I have never cared much for criticism of literature that tries to examine it from a theoretical construct (Marxist or feminist, for example) or—at the opposite extreme—objectively, as a thing-in-itself. Throughout my decades as a teacher of creative writing as well as of literature, I kept in mind three questions that, though attributed to Goethe, are basic enough to have a likely earlier source: What is the author trying to do? How well does he or she do it? Is it worth doing? One owes the work of any dedicated writer, aspiring or widely-known, the respect implied by the first two questions. The third, of course, is the difficult one, and must be answered with care. How can anybody properly address it? As a thing-in-itself, a work may have achieved its author's intent, but that doesn't necessarily make it beautiful or worthy of attention. If, in your respect for the specific work, you refuse to impose upon it a theoretical or any other limiting intellectual construct, your answer is bound to be subjective, dependent upon the previous literary works your reading has led you to admire as well as all the other attitudes and values provided by the experiences and cultural environment of your life. (Here, of course, I am circling back to the paradox described in the preface of this book.)

This is surely true of my responses to other writers, and accounts for my continuing references in this section to that long-ago winter night. Everybody has his or her reason for liking certain kinds of literature above others. The literary works that I most admire—the ones to my mind most "worth doing"—contain at their creative core the same kind of unifying impulse that first motivated me to turn to autobiographical essays as a consequence of that night early in the Cold War.

I have preceded some of the essays in this section on literature with brief notes that discuss the circumstances of their composition.

4   On Being Human

In 1936, I read Christopher Morley's *Human Being,* a book that is, at least for its time, unusual. It's a literary hybrid, the result of a coupling between a pair of more conventional forms—the novel and the essay. I was moved enough by that reading to carry over the decades a memory of its effect upon me, though I've never come across a mention of it.

In rereading *Human Being* after a passage of sixty-six years, I was surprised to discover that it had served as a guidepost to my future as teacher, critic, and writer—for that matter, to the self that at fifteen was uncertain of what it might become. My memory, stimulated by this new encounter with a book from my adolescence, found its own shape, or gestalt—one that links literary influences to nonliterary ones.

A comment by another writer provides me a better introduction to the shape of my thoughts and feelings than would any quotation I might extract from *Human Being.* It is from a series of lectures on the novel given by the English writer E. M. Forster at Cambridge University in

1927; *Aspects of the Novel,* the book that made the series available to a wider public, was published the same year. "Pattern and Rhythm" is the subject of the last lecture, and its final paragraph contains these words:

> Human beings have their great chance in the novel. They say to the novelist: "Recreate us if you like, but we must come in," and the novelist's problem, as we have seen all along, is to give them a good run and to achieve something else at the same time. Whither shall he turn? Not indeed for help but for analogy. Music, though it does not employ human beings, though it is governed by intricate laws, nevertheless does offer in its final expression a type of beauty which fiction might achieve in its own way. Expansion. That is the idea the novelist must cling to. Not completion. Not rounding off but opening out. When the symphony is over we feel that the notes and tunes composing it have been liberated, they have found in the rhythm of the whole their individual freedom. Cannot the novel be like that?

I was six years old in 1927, a first-grade student at P.S. 99 in Kew Gardens on Long Island, and already a reader. Of course, I never would have read a book like *Aspects of the Novel* at such an age, and, had I by chance come across that passage from it, I wouldn't have had the slightest idea of what the author was talking about. My parents had given me a subscription to a magazine called *The American Boy* that year, though, and I still remember the effect some of its fiction had on me. The substance of these stories has escaped my memory—which is not surprising, since seventy-five years have passed since I read them. But I do recall that a parade takes place near the end of one story—

people are marching down a street, and a band is playing while spectators cheer. Are these festivities in honor of the boy who is protagonist of the account? I no longer can answer that question, but in my memory some grand tune is playing still, a victory has been gained, and I have been subsumed into something larger than myself. This suggests (at least to me) that a child doesn't require the developing thematic interrelationships of Beethoven's Fifth Symphony, the musical parallel that Forster has in mind, or the vast geography of *War and Peace,* a novel he mentions in an earlier lecture, to gain the kind of expansion beyond the work that he was suggesting the novelist should strive for. (He may have been remembering—I find this likely—his own aspirations in *A Passage to India,* a novel for which Helen Schlegel's famous response to Beethoven's most popular symphony, in Forster's preceding novel, *Howards End,* provides a kind of advance gloss.)

I have no recollection of learning to read; unlike learning to write in script, it seems to have been an effortless process, as it must have been for many other children in those pre-Depression years when movies were still silent and radio was in its infancy. (We had few books in our Kew Gardens apartment, but we did have a battery-operated Atwater Kent radio with a speaker that resembled a fluted megaphone or huge shell. But nobody listened to it much, for the most impressive sounds it made were shrieks and whistles as the dial was turned.)

Always in quest of a better position, no matter how well-paying the present one might be, my father took his family from city to city throughout my childhood. (He was such a successful salesman of automobiles and pneumatic tires during the period of increasing demand for these relatively new commodities that he became a friend of Paul Hoffman, who ran the Studebaker corporation, and dined in Delaware with members of the Du Pont family, who once manufactured cars. I remember such names, for I was in awe of my father's achievements.) We had recently moved to Long Island from Milwaukee, and though my brother, who was ten, was old enough to have made some new friends, I had not, and my father was seldom home. In a way, *The American Boy* was my companion, my first friend.

We lived in that Long Island apartment only for a year; we moved in 1928 to Lakewood, a suburb of Cleveland, remaining in the same house for two years, which made it the longest-lasting location of my childhood. Our house was only a couple of blocks from that of my aunt and uncle and their two daughters. Unlike my parents, my uncle and aunt read books, and had filled one living-room wall with shelves of them; they lent me the first novel I remember reading. Though not a novel for children, Kipling's *The Light That Failed* opens with brief scenes about a childhood relationship between a boy and a girl, and perhaps that opening enticed me to read on. What I chiefly remember carrying away from that reading was a more complex desire than I'd known—an intense longing with sadness at its core—as its now-blinded hero, an artist, dies in an expanse of sand, having lost everything but his wish to die like that, from an enemy bullet in a foreign land. My bedroom window overlooked the wall of a long series of garages for tenants of the neighboring apartment building. The white-painted siding of that wall glowed with the soft golden radiance that a setting sun imparts to the humblest of objects. Probably I was in bed at that time of day because I was sick. But I remember nothing about that illness. I remember a longing and a grief that at the time had nothing to do with me, and I remember the reflected glow of the setting sun on a garage wall.

Though the fiction I read during my childhood was extraordinarily varied—westerns like Owen Wister's *The Virginian* and romances like Anthony Hope's *The Prisoner of Zenda,* most of the collected works of Mark Twain, *Moby-Dick,* and the science fiction of pulp magazines—no other novel would affect me like that until I was in the tenth grade in 1936. It seemed then as if the Depression would never end. My father had long since deserted the family and remarried. My brother, Jack, had been admitted to General Motors Institute, in Flint, Michigan, and my mother and I were living with him in a second-floor apartment near the business district. That institute was an engineering college in which the students combined their studies with practical experience in one of the large General Motors factories in Flint; the pay for the work covered tuition and living expenses. We were trying to get by on Jack's salary. It wasn't enough for food and rent for the three of us, and so we remained together for only a few months. (My mother was to find employment as a maid for a well-to-do widow, a distant relative, in Ohio, while I was to stay—briefly and unhappily—with my father and his second wife in Chicago. We lived in one of those sky-scraper apartments near the lake until, evicted for not paying the rent, we moved to smaller, shabbier quarters. My father had been unable to save a failing Packard dealership, and the inheritance the new wife had brought to the marriage was depleted. The marriage itself soon would end.)

In writing the above paragraph, I was surprised by the intensity of the feelings that accompanied my recall of those months in Flint. Had I known then that eventually my parents would be reunited, that period—long enough for me to attend only the fall semester at Flint's Central High School—would not have returned to me as such a rich but painful idyll. I longed for my father's return, for his absence had increased the sense of how much I loved him; but he had betrayed us, seemingly forever. I loved and respected my brother, who to the best of his ability was supporting us. But my deepest love was for my mother. Her own parents had died while she was still a child, and she had undergone what I now recognize as an almost Dickensian childhood, a victim of abuse from uncaring relatives and others who took her in. As I can tell from the photographs in my possession, she was, as a young woman, unusually lovely; but she did not marry until she was thirty-three. My father was only twenty at the time of their marriage. She was thirty-eight when I was born, and so was older than the mother of any of my classmates. Her hair remained reddish brown, though, until she learned my father wanted a divorce; in the following few months, it became white. Nothing in their relationship—always an affectionate one—had prepared her for that renunciation of it. But she possessed a loyalty that no betrayal could diminish. Having given her love to my father, she would never retract it. She never criticized him, and was hurt when I did.

On Being Human

I had brought to Flint three possessions, all of them gifts from my father: a dog, a bicycle, and a typewriter. Our landlady in Flint objected to the dog—Bruin, a large German shepherd, given to me when he was still a puppy —and Jack made the sturdy crate that sent him by Railway Express to my father's sister and her husband. I traded the bicycle at a second-hand store for an oval-shaped table radio. That was my Christmas present to my brother and mother; it was given in advance of the holiday, so that my mother could listen to the religious music of the season that she always enjoyed. (Of course it gave me a sense of nobility to do that, even though I had no use for the bicycle and I could listen to the radio, too. Jack was far too busy for that.) I kept the typewriter. It was a tiny Smith-Corona portable, its name and place of manufacture— Groton, N.Y.—inscribed on it in golden letters. (Groton, which lost its major source of income when Smith-Corona suspended operations there, is a village less than twenty miles away from my home of forty years, the farmhouse in which my wife and I reared our children. The enchanted Groton of my dreams, though, is not to be found on any map.) Without those particular months in Flint, and without that particular typewriter, I might never have become a writer. With them, I began to write story after story, hoping (among other vain hopes) to earn enough money to permit the three of us to stay together.

Expansion, Forster suggests, results from the "something else" that novelists in one way or another must bring to their narratives about people. This sense of expansion, coming after the completion of the work, obviously requires the imaginative participation of the reader, since it takes place within his or her mind. In Flint, the book in which I cooperated with the author to achieve such an effect was Christopher Morley's *Human Being*. One shelf of Central High School's library held a number of Morley's other works, all of which I read that semester— *Parnassus on Wheels, The Haunted Bookshop, Tales from a Roll-top Desk, Where the Blue Begins,* and *Thunder on the Left*— before I began *Human Being*. Playfulness and fantasy replace any attempt at realistic depiction in most of these books; I was delighted to discover that the protagonist of *Where the Blue Begins* is a dog. What *Human Being* shares with the others is a tolerance, an interest in the subject of books, and—above all else—a benign authorial presence.

The subtitle of *Human Being* is "A Story." (Morley must not have wanted it to carry the normal expectations of a novel, though it surely becomes one.) The central character is named Richard Roe, an indication that he is a generic figure; as the title suggests, he is simply a human being, one with no particular claims upon our attention. In the first chapter, Lawrence Hubbard, one of the narrators of the novel—the other and more pervasive narrator, has no name; he is what I recognized from my earlier readings to be Morley's own presence—meets Roe by chance, at a luncheon. From that encounter, he remembers little but a remark Roe had made: "Not long ago, I went up Riverside Drive at night on a bus. Suddenly an electric sign across the river flashed on in the dark, caught me right in the eyeball. It said THE TIME IS NOW 7:59. You know that damned thing frightened me." The second chapter opens with a brief newspaper notice of Roe's death on the Manhattan-to-Hoboken ferry, a victim neither of vengeance nor crime, but of an apparent heart attack.

To Hubbard, death lends an importance to his few memories of Roe, an unassuming figure he otherwise would have soon dismissed as simply another passing face on the sea of anonymity that is Manhattan. Is it simply whimsy—a kind of quixotic impulse—that determines Hubbard to save Roe from oblivion by searching for the humble details of his life that would constitute a biography, or is it Hubbard's justification—given our common human fate—for his own unexceptional life? At fifteen, I asked no questions like that. Increasingly, I was drawn to Richard Roe, but I was haunted by the fact that Morley was bringing back to life a person his text had declared to be dead: had Roe been granted this new life only to have it taken it away from him again? Perhaps everything I was reading was, like *Where the Blue Begins,* a fantasy with the kind of happy resolution I had imposed upon the busy plots of my own brief and implausible fictions. I held to that hope, despite the growing indications that Roe has physical problems, until I neared the conclusion. Of course he dies, crossing his River Styx while aboard that evening ferry to Hoboken.

It was night—as late as midnight, perhaps—when I finished the book. My mother might have been sleeping, my brother still studying at the desk in his bedroom; I remember nothing about that. Through the window, I could see thick flakes of snow illuminated by the street light at the corner of our block. How impossible it is to isolate any moment of the past from later as well as earlier memories! For my mind can't separate my responses to

The American Boy and *The Light that Failed* from my feelings that night any more than it can my responses to Joyce's *The Dead,* a story I first read twenty years later but whose ending now represents everything that night holds for me.

Unlike Joyce's Gabriel Conroy, who remains in the darkened hotel room looking outward at the snow falling through the lamplight, aware that it is descending everywhere—on land and water, on all the living and dead—I put on my jacket and took a long and aimless walk. Flint was in a tumultuous period of its history, for the CIO—its merger with the AFL years away—was in a battle to organize General Motors' factory workers; but the neighborhood streets I walked that night were deserted and silent. In speaking of himself, Richard Roe comments that he is chiefly known as the person who always gets bested by John Doe in sample contracts. Roe belonged to the generation of my parents. I knew that my father didn't believe in his own ordinariness—but then, who does? I had never thought of myself as ordinary; but I could see that in a way I was, as was everybody I loved; and the same was true of every man, woman, and child asleep in the darkened houses I passed. The compassion that his insight brings to Gabriel Conroy doesn't leave out pity for himself (doesn't the first word in the sentence "Generous tears filled Gabriel's eyes" carry a double meaning?) and probably mine didn't, either. All I can now say is that, throughout my long walk, the snow continued to fall.

Few people today have heard of Christopher Morley's *Human Being;* in order to reread it, I had to request its retrieval from Cornell University's computerized archival warehouse at the edge of the campus. Morley was born in 1890 and died in 1957; the novel, published in 1932, corresponds to a locale and a period (mainly Manhattan, from the early years of the last century through World War I and into the Depression) familiar to him. The growing affection I felt for Richard Roe comes in part from Morley's own obvious affection for particular places in New York City that Roe (often a lonely walker: his marriage is not a happy one) likes to revisit. Roe himself has affection for his wife and daughter, and his impulses remain generous throughout his life. Lucille, however, is anything but generous (her husband is valuable to her only to the extent that he is capable of improving her social status, particularly in reference to that of her sister), and she influences her daughter to share her growing disregard and contempt for Richard. Until the last days of World War I, he earns his living as a travelling salesman for a book publisher; he shares enough of the general optimism and dreams of the heady period that follows to form a small company that markets pens and desktop novelties of his devising. The success of that business—so necessary to Lucille's sense of status—depends on the woman Roe has hired to assist him. Minnie Hutzler has all the virtues that Lucille lacks—independence, imagination, practicality, a freedom from social conventions. Loving Richard, she becomes his mistress, wanting to do everything in her power to help him, even ending their intimacy in a futile attempt to save the marriage that he is unwilling to renounce.

In rereading the novel, I found the contrast between the two women—Lucille is nothing but a stereotype, after all—a blatant attempt to win my sympathy for Roe.

Could it be that Morley had made Roe's infidelity so understandable that it helped me as an adolescent to accept my father's behavior? Roe and my father had similar occupations, and each was influenced by the spirit of the 1920s that ended with the Depression. Given the vast difference between Lucille and my mother, though, it seems unlikely that I ever could have used Roe to explain my father. (In my later years, another fictional character, Jay Gatsby, would provide me a better, if still inadequate, analogy.)

While discussing fictional characters in *Aspects of the Novel,* Forster says it is permissible for a writer to take the reader into "confidence about the universe. . . . It is confidences about the individual people that do harm, and beckon the reader away from the people to an examination of the novelist's mind." Actually, what I found most appealing about that book *was* that mind, as revealed through the authorial presence; and while it does on occasion take the universe into account, it frequently confides in the reader about the people. For example, it includes a generalization about individuals like Richard Roe, each of whom can be seen as, in Morley's phrase, an "Unknown Citizen." We are told that "the most astounding achievement of society has been to train millions of people to think they believe certain ideas which they often don't believe at all." This "Unknown Citizen" would be appalled to hear himself declaring in public his views on subjects as various as "the Church, submarines, Russia, or the bringing up of children." Indeed, this citizen "had been silent so long about his innermost decencies he had almost forgotten they were there."

We learn, in advance of this generalization, that even though Richard's "glands reacted strongly to some injection of patriotic adrenalin by cartoon or editorial . . . , he felt there was something wrong somewhere." Afterward, we discover that the Museum of Natural History is particularly conducive to his doubts about what he is told he must believe. Within the Museum, he feels more religious than he does in church, finding the section of a 1400-year-old sequoia "more awful than a cathedral altar. . . . He could almost pray to that huge slab of smooth brown timber: it was a symbol of purity and patience."

Alas, in rereading such generalizations, I sense a condescension that is embedded within their very kindliness and warmth, and lends sentimentality even to views I share. This condescension may be faint, as in the example above; it is much more apparent in observations about women in general. What Morley says in his generalizations about women may apply, directly or indirectly, to Lucille and her sister, but they certainly don't to Minnie or any of the other women, young or old, whom he describes. Unlike the rest of the novel, these generalizations have a dated quality about them; representing as they do conventional attitudes of the period, they suggest that Morley is not immune to the social influences that shape the opinions of Roe or any other "Unknown Citizen."

As a genre, it is the personal essay and not the novel that readily gives freedom to the author's presence and permits it to give value to the small details of life. Though *Human Being* transforms itself into a novel by bringing the various strands together at the end, it is more essayistic than fictional in nature. Much like a personal essay based on memory, it dispenses with chronology and hence with a narrative sequence; though my summary of it might suggest otherwise, it has no plot in the conventional sense. Descriptions of Roe's apartment, of his train trips and encounters as a book salesman, and of the staff and atmosphere of his business offices in the Flatiron Building lend authenticity to his portrayal. Details, not the predicaments of plot, account for the reader's growing empathy with the protagonist. At fifteen, I liked Morley's method, and I still do. In Flint, the author's presence in arranging and coloring these details held my attention as much as did my desire for Richard Roe to stay alive.

Like other of my experiences during those months in Flint, my reading of that book is linked to my later life. I discovered E. M. Forster only after I was married and discharged from the Army following the conclusion of World War II. Morley had introduced me to the pleasures and dimension that a writer's presence can give; and it was Forster's clear and yet more elusive presence that first drew me to his novels. Forster's plots often seem contrived to serve other ends; still, he is more successful than Morley in attaching his presence to the ongoing narrative. In *Aspects of the Novel,* Forster is far less interested in the matter of presence than in a quality that, while obviously coming from it, implies a unity beyond personality: the presence becomes anonymous, a "prophetic voice."

In our own splintered and less credulous age, the belief that literature can communicate a sense of universality beyond singularity or authorial presence has lost much of its strength. But the power of literature, it seems to me, still lies in its imaginative ability to imply a realm beyond our grasp; by transcending the limitations of reader, character, and society, it can give us an awareness of our human mutuality. Unlike Forster, most of us think of "presence" and "voice" as synonyms; in the creative works I most admire, they do coalesce, even in his terms. The first book I published was an attempt to define Forster's presence in his novels—a presence that serves as a mediator between opposing positions, between those of matter and spirit, between the "seen" and the "unseen" realms, and in so doing becomes a voice; and I used his own book on the novel as a guide. Later in life, I transferred my major affection to Chekhov. He seems—he is—a more objective writer than Forster, and yet I can sense his presence in his stories and plays: it is apparent even through the gauze of the various translations I depend upon. While undeniably *there,* that presence is even more elusive than Forster's, whatever the affinities between them; it is as elusive as it is because it, too, is after something beyond the writer himself—and so would be anonymous. Chekhov had no luck with novels, and destroyed his attempts to write them. But he doesn't need the complications and dramatic struggles of a long form to achieve his effects. His presence in his stories seems to be one with the Chekhov who lived outside them. How does one describe a presence so united with the sensibility and life of its author that it can't be examined simply within the frame of a work of art? As best as I can describe it, Chekhov's presence—his voice—wishes to escape the confines of self and society; its desire for an unobtainable freedom is reflected in its compassion for the major characters its author constructs, whose traps sometimes are of their own willful making. To put it another way, we humans are different from each other, and yet alike—and are to be valued as spiritual as well as material beings with the kind of longings that always must elude their achievement in the physical world. (My father had longings never to be fulfilled, and so does Morley's Richard Roe and Forster's Fielding, the protagonist of his finest novel, *A Passage to India*. Who, real or imagined, does not?) And so I wrote a book about Chekhov's major adventure, his long and lonely journey across Siberia to the prison colony on Sakhalin Island, using it and every other means at my disposal to define his presence, indistinguishable as it is from his voice.

We are what we were, as our memories can tell us. What I read at six or eight or fifteen is part of what I now am, as reflected in all of my writing; and I am more indebted to Christopher Morley—my rereading of *Human Being* has proved that to me—than I had known. The form most congenial to me has long been the autobiographical essay, its subject the ordinary details of a past that memory reconstructs from a present event.

Within the personal essay, subject is inseparable from authorial presence. Still, my dislike for the first person singular is pronounced, and I would be unable to use it imaginatively if I didn't consider myself representative rather than unique, as generic a figure as Richard Roe; in a sense, as a fictional character whose author is after the "something else" that all of us want—in life as well as in the fiction we read.

5 Two Anonymous Writers:
E. M. Forster and Anton Chekhov

I wrote this essay at the request of the editors who were assembling material for a book on E. M. Forster in celebration of his centenary. That book, E. M. Forster: A Human Exploration, *was published in 1979. In writing the essay about my rereading of Christopher Morley's* Human Being *that opens this section, I was unaware of the affinity between its concluding pages and "Two Anonymous Writers." (The latter essay was written almost 25 years before the former; in the intervening years I had lost both the manuscript copy of "Two Anonymous Writers" and the book in which it was published. Fortunately, the Cornell library had a copy of that book.) I was surprised to discover how faithful my memory has been to the values I found in Forster, and re-found in Chekhov, and which have their antecedent—as the first essay in this section finds—in my life and reading as a child and adolescent.*

The biography of Forster referred to in "Two Anonymous Writers" is volume I of P. N. Furbank's E. M. Forster: A Life, *published in 1979. Volume II, though published the following year, was not yet available at the time I wrote my essay.*

E. M. Forster requires in his readers a greater personal stability than do many writers, for he appeals even in his youthful fiction to our inclination to reflect on our own experiences as well as to our wish for wholeness and wisdom. I know I didn't discover him until I was back from service in the Second World War, beginning a career, and feeling more secure in my sexual and spiritual nature than I had as an adolescent or soldier. What I found in him were a number of qualities I had responded to in my childhood and adolescent reading—fantasy, humor, compassion, a loneliness connected with both a sense of foreign places and a desire for something beyond one's apparent grasp—all of these qualities transformed or given perspective by an authorial presence that, while it forbade the self-indulgence of my adolescent responses, permitted an understanding of the failings of specific human beings as well as of the limitations of the human condition itself. I first read Forster in my mid-twenties, a period in which a certain kind of imaginative literature can influence us for the rest of our lives; to a considerable extent the authorial presence in his fiction became (to misuse the common definition of the phrase) *my* second self, and so it has remained to the present day.

In reading the recently published first volume of P. N. Furbank's projected two-volume biography of Forster, I found myself as fascinated by it as I had been by the books of my childhood; I read it with a kind of wonder at the distance separating the details and anxieties of the life from the knowledge found in the fiction. Forster was frank and honest about himself in his personal notations, which is as admirable as it is uncommon; but the biography, dependent as it is on its subject's candor, manages to be, like Alice's rabbit-hole, a means of enchanted diminution. The Cambridge of the *Life* is a tinier place than is the Cambridge of *The Longest Journey;* the Italy of the *Life* is far more confining than is the Italy of *Where Angels Fear to Tread* and *A Room with a View,* the intimacy with specific Italians in the *Life* apparently being limited to lessons with a language teacher. How lonely, how unfulfilled, Forster must have been—later, in England—to seek out male companionship in various disagreeable locales! As we journey through the *Life,* the Baedeker we require to point out the spirit of Forster—to define the inner life, to provide stars for the grand vistas—consists of the novels and stories and essays he wrote.

The publication in England of this first volume of the *Life,* coming in advance of the hundredth anniversary of his birth and after the appearance of the homosexual fiction, will inevitably bring about the demand for a re-evaluation of Forster from a variety of psychological perspectives. Attempts in this direction are bound to be reductive even as they celebrate complexity. Forster himself knew better than to rely on the methods of any science of the mind for an understanding of who and what we are. His own best characters are simple but not flat, for he seeks the depths rather than the intricacies; his fiction is remarkably free of the more popular terms of psychology, even in defining a character so vulnerable to them as Adela Quested. In *Aspects of the Novel,* while discussing the qualities of Melville's mind, Forster writes, "What one notices in him is that his apprehensions are free from personal worry, so that we become bigger, not smaller, after sharing them;" and, in general, the comment is applicable to Forster himself, to the presence inhabiting his fiction. The major exception is *Maurice*. In that novel, the presence, while there, is muted for the sake of the argument. If allowed its normal play, that presence would have implied a base in Maurice deeper than his homosexuality, and would have severely undercut the intention to give him happiness once he had openly accepted his sexual nature —much as it undercuts conscious intentions, thereby preventing them from becoming sentimental, in most of the other novels.

But of course "authorial presence" is too restrictive a term to describe what we respond to in Forster's writing, as we listen to whatever it is that lies behind the character and between the words and the structural blocks. It used to bother me when I was younger that my favorite author, whose accents were so familiar to me that I felt him to be my friend, would subscribe to the notion of anonymity in literature—a notion quite fashionable in the forties and fifties, for it was in keeping with the views of the New Criticism. His remarks in "Anonymity: An Enquiry" bothered me because I wasn't attending to them properly; words so simply put have to be felt in our entire psyche, not just the reasoning part. What he was saying in that essay I had to discover for myself, as a truth about my own nature, though his words are so clear a child *should,* by natural right, be able to understand them:

> Just as words have two functions—information and creation—so each human mind has two personalities, one on the surface, one deeper down. The upper personality has a name. It is called S.T. Coleridge, or William Shake-

speare, or Mrs. Humphry Ward. It is conscious and alert, it does things like dining out, answering letters, etc., and it differs vividly and amusingly from other personalities. The lower personality is a very queer affair. In many ways it is a perfect fool, but without it there is no literature, because unless a man dips a bucket down into it occasionally he cannot produce first-class work. There is something general about it. Although it is inside S. T. Coleridge, it cannot be labelled with his name. It has something in common with all other deeper personalities, and the mystic will assert that the common quality is God, and that here, in the obscure recesses of our being, we near the gates of the Divine. It is in any case the force that makes for anonymity. As it came from the depths, so it soars to the heights, out of local questionings; as it is general to all men, so the works it inspires have something general about them, namely beauty.

Later in this lucid essay—one that moves me as much as do the finest passages in his novels—Forster makes some comments that ought to be read by any reader of *E. M. Forster: A Life:*

The personality of a writer does become important after we have read his book and begin to study it. When the glamour of creation ceases, when the leaves of the divine tree are silent, when the co-partnership [between reader and writer] is over, then a book changes its nature, and we can ask ourselves questions about it such as 'What is the author's name?' 'Where did he live?' 'Was he married?' and 'Which was his favourite flower?' Then we are no longer reading the book, we are studying it and making it subserve our desire for information. 'Study' has a very solemn sound. 'I am studying Dante' sounds much more than 'I am reading Dante.' It is really much less. Study is only a serious form of gossip. It teaches us everything about the book except the central thing, and between that and us it raises a circular barrier which only the wings of the spirit can cross.

As for the passage about the two personalities upon which this second quotation depends—either we understand it fully, or we don't understand it at all. In rereading "Anonymity" some twenty years after I'd last read it, I was surprised, disconcerted, and finally delighted to find that the attitudes toward the acts of reading and writing I had been slowly developing over the years, as well as the two critical terms that had become of crucial importance to me in explaining these attitudes to others, actually had their specific origins in this essay and their general origins in Forster's fiction and other writings. What is *tone,* after all, but the attitudes communicated to us by the upper personality? What is *voice* but our apprehension of the lower? We can say that "authorial presence" accommodates both tone and voice, but only if we are willing to admit that the latter term is subversive. In *Aspects of the Novel,* Forster refers to prophecy as a quality of voice. Prophecy is a consequence of the power of voice to invoke the general and universal at the expense of the personal and idiosyncratic; tone, as I would use the word, belongs to the realm of the personal and idiosyncratic.

Two questions are apt to trouble the reader of "Anonymity" who does not immediately accede to the truth it contains. The first, which is easier to meet, has to do with the somewhat guarded nature of its comments about

mysticism. Isn't Forster at once appealing to our acceptance of the mystic truth at the heart of any number of religions (". . . the mystic will assert that the common quality is God") *and* sidestepping his own acceptance of such
truth? Between the two passages I have quoted, and as
part of his bridge between them, Forster speaks regretfully
of the loss of the old theories of composition that permitted literature to be "not an expression but a discovery,
and was sometimes supposed to have been shown to the
poet by God."

The first question, then, takes on the form of "How serious is Forster? Does he really believe what he says?" The
answer, of course, is that he is wholly serious, that he does
believe in something called the "soul" or the "spirit" of
man; that, in speaking of "a circular barrier which only the
wings of the spirit can cross" he is not speaking sentimen-
tally or decoratively. Few humans—certainly none of
those engaged in the acts of reading and writing—are simple receptacles to be filled up with the divine message; we
are not the bucket itself. And yet individually we do possess
a lower personality: it is what we have in common. His fiction everywhere depends on the assumptions of "Anonymity," as does all literature that relies on heightened moments in which the self or the individual consciousness
recedes or pales before an apprehension of unity.

The second question, which I once asked and which
some critics of Forster still are asking, seems to involve us
in a paradox. The question is: "If the greatest literature is
that in which the author most closely approximates
anonymity, if in it the writer moves himself or herself and

us through the extinction of 'presence,' of individual ego, why is it that in that literature we hear certain distinct and unique accents and thus can clearly distinguish those of Melville from those, say, of Dostoevsky or Emily Brontë —something that we can't do for any number of lesser writers?"

"Anonymity" can answer this question, too. The movement toward anonymity through the lower personality *does* provide a closer relationship between reader and writer than is possible without it; they are drawn together at the level that truly matters, the level beneath differences of race, nationality, sex, politics, culture, and quirky individualism. Sometimes ideas are so simple it takes us half a century to comprehend them; they are the sort of ideas once accepted without much thought and sometimes without much comprehension as belonging to the matrix of the religious doctrines of the age. The value of struggling for them without the benefit of creed and orthodoxy is that one can finally get to them without their robes on, can see them in their elemental form. It took me nearly five decades to realize that the personality—the separate identity—I prize in others and in myself would be devoid of meaning or value did I not somehow *know* that a point exists in which all these diverse selves merge, become one. What significance (we must stand outside of our private lives and the world we subjectively create to ask this question) could there possibly be in our separate opinions, our lonely desires, the glint of intelligence in our eyes, the very pattern of our thumbprints, without such a point? And isn't it obvious that all writers who find their essential interest in a person or persons and not in the relationship of individuals to human institutions accept, whether they are conscious of the fact or not, this final point of convergence?

Our lower personality—the writer's voice—acknowledges such a point; and, by giving us in the process our common value, makes meaningful communication at least a possibility. Our higher personality—the writer's tone—can think and talk (usually unsuccessfully) about that point beyond words, is consciously affected or unconsciously influenced by it in varying degrees even as it is engaged in classifying, declaring one thing or idea better than another, or performing the mundane activities that Forster ascribes to it.

It is true, I feel, that the lower personality would, if left unchecked, lose itself wholly in that silence that for Augustine is the voice of God. Writers of fiction, however, work of necessity with human beings, and such a concern serves—as did the example of Christ for Augustine—to pull even the most prophetic of them back to Earth. In the writing in which we are most aware of such a dual allegiance, the characters ultimately are defined not in social or material terms but in spiritual ones.

Here is Forster's younger contemporary and friend, Virginia Woolf, on a writer whose name for a moment will remain, fittingly enough, anonymous:

> We have to cast about in order to discover where the emphasis in these strange stories rightly comes. X's own words give us a lead in the right direction. ". . . [S]uch a conversation as this between us," he says, "would have

been unthinkable for our parents. At night they did not talk, but slept sound; we, our generation, sleep badly, are restless, but talk a great deal, and are always trying to settle whether we are right or not." Our literature of social satire and psychological finesse both sprang from that restless sleep, incessant talking; but, after all, there is an enormous difference between X and Henry James, between X and Bernard Shaw. Obviously—but where does it arise? X, too, is aware of the evils and injustices of the social state; the condition of the peasants appals him, but the reformer's zeal is not his—that is not the signal for us to stop. The mind interests him enormously; he is a most subtle and delicate analyst of human relations. But again, no; the end is not there. Is it that he is primarily interested not in the soul's relation with other souls, but with the soul's relation to health—with the soul's relation to goodness? These stories are always showing us some affectation, pose, insincerity. Some woman has got into a false relation; some man has been perverted by the inhumanity of his circumstances. The soul is ill; the soul is cured; the soul is not cured. Those are the emphatic points in his stories.

Such a description—except for the quotation, which tells us that X simply has to be Russian: the English never generalize so freely about their spiritual complaints— could easily be of Forster's fiction, but Woolf is speaking of Chekhov.

In his letters, Chekhov talks readily enough about his personal feelings, but in his fiction his characters rather than he are open. He tries always in his stories to be impersonal, objective, though he does generalize about man's relationship with the universe, about the vastness of space and the loneliness and ephemerality of the human condition—those generalizations that Forster in *Aspects of the Novel* approves of, partly, I suspect, because they have their source in the lower personality. Chekhov, though, does construct characters that represent the elements of his own nature.

In this regard, no more telling story exists than "Gusev," a brief piece of fiction that Woolf praises in her essay "Modern Fiction." It is the account of two men who die as a ship slowly makes its homeward way to Russia. Gusev himself is simple, accepting everything and everybody in his world but the Chinese. He makes no intellectual distinctions, no moral categories; folk tales and myths, no matter how superstitious, satisfy his need for explanation. He may be, from the rationalist's point of view (and that is the viewpoint of the other character) a perfect fool, but he is also soul, the lower personality—without ever becoming a symbol. The other dying man, Pavel Ivanych, is constantly aware of classes, divisions—and of himself. He is outraged at human injustice, but not because he is compassionate—rather, because he sees it in reference to his personal suffering. He too is not a symbol, he is a particular man, Pavel Ivanych. He is also (in contrast to soul) body, which reason serves for body's own ends; he is the higher personality untouched by any knowledge of the lower.

The deaths of both men are described in the most laconic and objective of terms, as is Gusev's sea burial. The only intrusions Chekhov permits himself come at the very end, as he describes what would be a physical impossibility for any human to see: the depths and the heights. He employs a kind of double vision, that is, to capture the realms of both water and sky—the substance and soul of a natural universe totally oblivious of any such division in it. Below, a shrouded body is sinking deeper and deeper into subterranean darkness, followed by pilot fish and a shark that finally rips the shroud; above, the clouds over the ocean are illuminated to a transcendent beauty by the light of the setting sun. The verbal intrusions, such as they are, consist of the attempt to give human emotions to the fish and ocean and to see the clouds as representations of familiar objects—a triumphal arch, a lion, something so homely as a pair of scissors. The attempt, in short, is to make the pathetic fallacy *work,* to impose as much human meaning as it is possible upon an indifferent natural world in which men as diverse as Gusev and Pavel Ivanych are treated exactly alike, in the fact of their dying; but the final emphasis is on a beauty and truth beyond words or human encompassment—even though there is one last attempt to describe nature as if it were man. "Looking at this magnificent enchanting sky"—so goes the last sentence—"the ocean frowns at first, but soon it, too, takes on tender, joyous, passionate colors for which it is hard to find a name in the language of man."

If I were to meet in person one of those people who sometimes grumble in print about *A Passage to India*—those who feel it to be an expression of fatigue, or who do not understand the importance of both the old fool Godbole and the rational but discontented Fielding, or who declare that since not even Godbole can encompass stone in his quest for unity the book is a novel of despair and nothing more—I would give that person this little Chekhov story to read in solitude, trusting to his or her psyche to make the necessary connections. I wish Woolf had re-read "Gusev" before she composed her often perceptive, but sometimes condescending, essay on Forster's novels.

No "name in the language of man" exists, of course, for that ultimate point of convergence, for the unifying Beauty or Truth beyond human consciousness; and both Forster and Chekhov disclaim knowledge of "Truth." Both of them have more skeptical intelligences than most prophetic writers do; like some writers of the eighteenth century, their very emphasis on reason makes them aware of its limits. The care with which they construct their sentences, with which they give structure to their works, is a sign of intelligence paying homage to a beauty beyond it and separates them from those who rely with more singleness of intent on the lower personality.

For most of his novelistic career—up to *A Passage to India*—Forster believed the greater unity beyond consciousness could at least be sensed through the natural flux, through a person's spiritual kinship with place, and that such an awareness could lead to a true connection among men. That this Wordsworthian view was for him an intellectual conviction or nostalgic desire merely, not the knowledge of the lower personality, is obvious in the disparity between what all the earlier novels say and what they imply—the disparity between tone and voice. It is possible that Forster's homosexuality—which, whatever his efforts, set him apart and gave him an immense need for a connection to be achieved with our bodies, on this Earth—accounts for such a thematic conviction; it is likely also that his English reasonableness for a long time demanded something tangible, something to be looked at and touched, as proof of what the lower personality already knew. In a similar way, Augustine's rationality caused him for some years to believe that God somehow must be an object, a material substance however diaphanous or permeable—or how else can we approach and love Him?

Unlike Forster, Chekhov never proposed nature as a solution for our spiritual cravings. The appeal to him of sky and steppe, of the immense landscapes of his native land, simply is in keeping with his impulse toward anonymity. In his stories, this impulse is reflected in his efforts to be as objective as possible. In his life, it is reflected in his continual desire for freedom, to escape from labels, social categories, political distinctions—and from pettiness and all the other imprisoning tendencies of his own ego. It is, we could say, the lower personality rebelling from the upper—the simple Gusev seeking freedom from that irksome Pavel Ivanych.

And yet that part of him which urges him toward an overcoming of self—which tells him of a unity beyond consciousness—that part of him permits, as it does with Forster, the moral concern: what finally matters is "the soul's relation to health . . . the soul's relation to goodness," with health and goodness always connected to what unifies us, as a community of human beings. The enemy —the evil—is that which is self-centered and self-seeking, arrogant, petty, divisive. The enemy can be any social force, any political or religious orthodoxy, that does injury to the person, that denies the implicit value of the individual for the sake of class or category or ideology; and it equally can be any imprisoning force within that individual.

As a young man I wrote a book about Forster's novels —it was my doctoral dissertation—that he liked enough to write a letter expressing his appreciation for the copy I had sent him. What he apparently liked most were the comments on *A Passage to India*. He took exception to my calling Stephen Wonham of *The Longest Journey* a minor character, for that was not what he had wanted Stephen to be—though he recognized that he had not shown, other than through Stephen's talk with Ansell, what he should have about him. In a postscript, he called attention to my error in referring to Eleanor Lavish of *A Room with a View* as Lydia: "Eleanor Lavish—not Lydia—but she would be too delighted to be mentioned at all to mind;" and in a second postscript he wrote, in reference to my wish in the letter accompanying the book, "Yes—I hope we meet some day."

If my one meeting with Forster, which finally took place in July 1963, when he was eighty-four, was not the disaster it might have been, the credit must go to his tolerance and kindness. In the note he had sent me in Paris, where I was spending the year with my family, he said King's would be deserted for the vacation and gave me simple directions for finding his rooms. I suppose the emptiness of the courtyard, lending the buildings a loveliness that belonged to the past, had something to do with my conversational ineptness. Also, upon climbing the stairs, I saw the faded paint of Forster's name on the door, and it immediately made me remember one of the many tokens of mutability in *The Longest Journey*—the fact that underneath Rickie Elliot's name on *his* door at that college lay the ghost of an earlier one. At any rate, Forster, upon answering my knock, looked to me so frail and elderly—he was recuperating from a heart attack—that my eyes filled with tears and I was even more incoherent than an educated Englishman expects the average American to be. Almost at once, I blurted out what I fear I said too often during my hour or so with him (and what these present recollections disprove somewhat): I said I came neither as a scholar nor critic, not for any *use* to which the meeting could be put, but simply to tell him his books had been one of the crucial influences upon my life.

He smiled and set about putting me to ease. He made tea—drawing water for the kettle, if I remember correctly, from the taps of an old-fashioned bathtub—and produced a cake. And, wanting to show an interest in me, he asked about my own writing—for surely the book about him could be but a small part of my literary efforts. Since at the time it constituted my chief writing accomplishment, the subject was quickly exhausted. For the sake of talk, he asked me which city I preferred—London or Paris. I said quickly, "Paris," for I knew it better and found a greater aesthetic delight both in its buildings and river; he told me that he had such a distaste for Paris—for the rudeness of its citizens—that he bypassed it on all his trips to the south of France. His current writing struck me as possibly a more profitable topic, so I asked him about it. He said he no longer was doing anything creative; his time now was taken up in going through all his papers and destroying everything he didn't want to linger after his death. I wanted to know what future he had in mind for the unpublished novel about homosexuality I had heard so much about. Quite firmly he said he had decided never to have it published; written primarily to protest attitudes that now had altered, the novel was both old-fashioned and lacking social justification.

For the greater part of our meeting, we talked about novels we both liked and novels he thought I would like, such as Mrs. Gaskell's *Wives and Daughters.* He expressed his low opinion of motion pictures generally but of his liking for the theater. Santha Rama Rau's stage adaptation of *A Passage to India* had pleased him. Toward the end of our conversation, and without connection with anything that had preceded it, he told me that as a young man he had made one major mistake. Of course I asked what that mistake had been; his reply, the only one I can remember accurately enough to put quotation marks around, was "I trusted people too much."

He waited for my response. Why was it that such a statement would shock and even embarrass me into silence? Why wasn't I wise or Russian enough to answer, at least to reveal something about myself? Instead I passed off what he said as best I could, saying something about how *A Passage to India* reminded me of the late quartets of Beethoven: I meant such a comparison to imply that I understood what he had said but that I was unable to cope directly with it. Actually, I had understood it only in my mind. My feelings told me I hadn't wanted an elderly man whom I had always admired to tell me anything like that; my feelings told me—wrongly—that it negated the importance of human relationships, including the one I had hoped to establish with him. He said at once he much preferred the early Beethoven to the late; my response clearly had been inadequate, and we were back to our original positions. As I prepared to leave, he said he would accompany me to the gate. Too solicitous, perhaps, of his health, I suggested he needn't do that. Almost acidly he said that he owed it to me, for my book.

And so he saw me down the stairs, over the uneven cobblestones of the courtyard where I feared he might fall, and over too an odd plank at the bottom of the open gate. I thanked him for his hospitality as he stood beside the ornate mail collection box—a reminder of the Victorian age, with the initials V. R. central to its iron embellishments. Because I didn't want to say goodbye, partly because something had gone wrong that still might be saved, I said what I felt at that instant. I said, "I like that mail box," meaning I liked seeing him there beside it. He said that he had always liked that pillar-box too; and he smiled warmly, as if in my departure we might yet be affectionate.

So much for the gossip of information that perhaps tells more about me than the ostensible subject. But as the years have passed, I have often thought of his phrase, *I trusted people too much*. For a time I was able to convince myself that it was intended as a kindly warning to me, the naive young American; and doubtless that was at least part of its intention. Those words most recently came to my mind in reading the first volume of Furbank's biography.

Had Forster been remembering the trust he had placed as a young man in Hugh Meredith and Syed Ross Masood and their betrayal of it?

But one doesn't really need these biographical details (which, being the biographer's interpretation, may or may not be correct) to understand such a remark by a truthful elderly man. All of us would, if we could, impart to the familiar world and to those whom we love the constancy and wholeness lying beyond the grasp of our consciousness. Chekhov's characters, struggling for an unobtainable happiness, lie again and again about the nature of that happiness, about themselves, and about those whom they would love: their self-deceptions prevent the degree of happiness that otherwise would be possible. In a somewhat similar fashion, Rickie Elliott, Forster's most autobiographical character, places a burden of trust on Agnes and particularly on Stephen that no human can bear. The seen and the unseen, the prose and the poetry, the upper personality and lower, the body and the soul, remain separate.

Although in his major essays Forster makes no reference to Chekhov, he did write a review in 1915 of two collections of Chekhov stories—a fact brought to my attention by Frederick P. W. McDowell, compiler of the recent annotated bibliography of writings on Forster, when he learned of my interest in discussing the two writers. In his review, Forster is wary of the reason—the English want all the information they can get about the national spirit of their wartime ally—for the sudden interest in Chekhov and other Russian writers. Chekhov provides no such information; he is concerned not with generalizations about the Russian people but with specific individuals and subjects. Chekhov is "both realist and poet. With one hand he collects facts; with the other he arranges them and sets them flowing." (Woolf later was to criticize that kind of ambidexterity in Forster's fiction, for she preferred fewer bricks and a more constant flowing.) Forster gives the following quotation from a Chekhov story to illustrate what he means:

> "In which country are the birds most at home, in ours or over there?" Savka asked.
>
> "In ours, of course. They are hatched here, and here they raise their young. This is their native land, and they only fly away to escape being frozen to death."
>
> "How strange!" he sighed, stretching. "One can't talk of anything but what is strange. Take that shouting bird over there, take people, take this little stone—there's a meaning in everything. Oh, if I had only known you were going to be here this evening, sir, I wouldn't have told that woman to come. She asked if she might."
>
> "These affairs of yours with women will end badly some day," I said sadly.
>
> "Never mind."
>
> Then, after a moment's reflection, Savka added:
>
> "So I have told the women, but they won't listen; the idiots don't care."
>
> Silence fell. The shadows deepened, the outlines of all objects faded into the darkness. The streak of light behind the hill was altogether extinguished, and the stars shone ever brighter and brighter. The mournful, monotonous chirping of the crickets, the calling of the rail-bird, and the whistling of the quail seemed not to break the nocturnal silence, but rather to add to it a still greater depth. It was as if the stars, and not the birds and insects,

were singing softly, and charming our ears as they looked down from heaven.

Savka broke silence first. He slowly turned his regard to me, and said, "This is tedious for you, sir, I can see. Let's have supper."

I find echoes of this scene in *A Passage to India;* indeed, part of its resonance for me comes from my knowledge of that novel. Effects somewhat similar to those found in this quotation—effects gained by the movement from the specific to the general or universal and then quickly back—can be found throughout Forster's fiction. But the affinities are the result of spiritual kinship, not of influence. Certainly it is the attraction of what lies beyond self, the attraction of an encompassing and holy silence, that gives to both Chekhov and Forster an elusiveness. I know that Forster led me to Chekhov and that Chekhov led me back to Forster. The process is similar to that in learning a foreign language: the study of it informs us of the workings of our native tongue by making accessible those crucial parts that both languages have in common. The voice in Forster and Chekhov alike is a mediator between seemingly irreconcilable elements, giving us what solace it can, reminding us of our likenesses, and telling us that oneness exists—but not now, not here.

6   A Faded Portrait

In the early 1990s, the editor of a literary journal sent me an as-yet-unpublished essay by Irving Howe about Chekhov's story "In the Cart." To Howe, that brief story—simple and transparent as it is—illustrates the limitations of literary theory or any kind of technical analysis. After summarizing the small actions that form the narrative thread of "In the Cart," Howe remarks that a phrase as nebulous as "Chekhov's spirit" is all that one can really say about a story that "is a small masterpiece." Actually, Howe's essay has a subversive intent, despite his long career as a critic whose literary concerns are connected to the need for social justice. He is using this story as a challenge to the nature of criticism itself; for no theory can address the quality that gives a literary work its unique value. The "spirit" underlying this little story is "undecipherable or perhaps better, ungraspable."

The editor of the journal sent Howe's essay to a number of distinguished critics as well as to me, for he considered that a challenge of this sort might provide a symposium of interest to readers; but my response was apparently the only one he received. "A Faded Portrait" wasn't difficult to write, since I'd already discussed, as best I could, the voice underlying Chekhov's creative work that is responsible for the "spirit" to be found everywhere within it. (The essay about Forster and Chekhov that precedes this one was followed in 1984 by my To a Distant Island, *which was, beyond all else, an attempt to define such an elusive matter.)*

Chekhov once wrote his friend and publisher, A. S. Suvorin, "The artist ought not to judge his characters or what they say, but be only an unbiased witness." And yet his work—as even such a brief example of it as "In the Cart" demonstrates—has a kind of spiritual or moral authority that permits us to know the difference between "good" and "bad," and to feel compassion for human suffering, whether self-induced or at the hands of another. In one of the most perceptive generalizations ever written about him—even though it is but part of an essay, "The Russian Point of View," published in 1925 in her *The Common Reader* (first series)—Virginia Woolf says that Chekhov

> is aware of the evils and injustices of the social state; the condition of the peasants appals him, but the reformer's zeal is not his—this is not the signal for us to stop. The mind interests him enormously; he is a most subtle and delicate analyst of human relations. But again, no; the end is not there. Is it that he is primarily interested not in the soul's relation with other souls, but with the soul's relation to health—with the soul's relation to goodness? These stories are always showing us some affectation, pose, insincerity. Some woman has got into a false relation; some man has been perverted by the inhumanity of his circumstances. The soul is ill; the soul is cured; the soul is not cured. Those are the emphatic points in his stories.

Chekhov had little use for religion; he rejected the Christianity of his day as superstition. Yet it seems appropriate to refer to the "souls" of his characters, and the relation of those souls to such matters as "health" and "goodness." In my own reading of Chekhov (as well as of my own psyche) the "soul" is but another term for the desire for freedom and unity that always must lie beyond our attainment. In a famous letter to his acquaintance Alexis Pleshcheyev on October 4, 1888, Chekhov writes, "I am neither liberal, nor conservative, nor gradualist, nor monk, nor indifferentist. . . . I look upon tags and labels as prejudices. My holy of holies is the human body, health, intelligence, talent, inspiration, love and the most absolute freedom imaginable, freedom from violence and lies, no matter what form the latter two take. Such is the program I would adhere to if I were a major artist."

Well, he was a major artist, one whose own metaphysical desire for such freedom becomes, in his creative work, a human constant, however deluded his characters may be—however much they act to impair the limited amount of freedom that they and others can obtain. What, though, is the source of that underlying desire for an unlimited freedom? In "Daydreams," a poignant 1886 story about the recapture of an escaped convict by two rural constables, the convict's description of the freedom that exists in the natural world of eastern Siberia—a region he has never seen, except in his dreaming—momentarily overwhelms the constables, mired in actual life as they are. "In the autumn stillness, when the chill, sullen mist that hangs over the earth weighs upon the heart, when it looms like a prison wall before the eyes, and bears witness to the limited scope of man's will, it is sweet to think of broad, swift rivers, with steep banks open to the sky, of impenetrable forests, of boundless plains," Chekhov writes, interpreting for us the constables' feelings. Then he adds, commenting on the constables from his own perspective in a way that in later stories he would mute or make more subtle: "The constables picture to themselves a free life such as they have never lived; whether they vaguely remember scenes from stories heard long ago or whether they have inherited notions of a free life from remote free ancestors with their flesh and blood, God alone knows!"

The desire for an unobtainable freedom, then, may possibly come from our genetic memories of life within nature—hypothesis or wild guess, this is the closest that Chekhov ever comes to suggesting an initial source for such a mystery. It is clear enough from his letters and his single major work of nonfiction, as well as his creative work, that vast natural vistas—steppes, forests, sky, water, mountain ranges—appealed to that desire within himself. That some deeply buried memory of freedom, whether genetic or not, underlies his characters seems likely from the very distortions or deceptions—the illusions of a past or future happiness—that give them their personalities. Howard Moss, in a fine essay on *Three Sisters* (it is included in his 1981 collection, *Whatever is Moving*) says, "The repeated sounding of 'Moscow!' is more than the never-to-be-reached Eldorado of the work or its lost Eden; it is a symbol of distance itself, that past or future in space from

which the characters are forever barred," and he goes on
to say that memory lures the men and women of the play
in opposing directions: the men want to stay in the present, mistaking it for the past, while the women "would do
anything, short of what is necessary, to be removed,"
wanting to find in the future the past "life they have lived
(they think)."

The crucial role played by memory is emphasized in
Chekhov's "In the Cart" through its loss. The story takes
place in April, as spring is replacing winter. The deadness
of winter is one with the deadness of Marya's soul; we are
told at the very beginning that the routine, the hardships,
of her thirteen years as a rural schoolmistress have so
blighted her psyche that she pays no attention to the natural transformation taking place, noticing not even "this
marvelous, immeasurably deep sky into which it seemed
that one would plunge with such joy." That is to say, desire itself is absent from her.

Chekhov may withhold judgments about his characters' actions, but is not adverse to carefully placed generalizations. A close reading of this story would have to take
into account all the passages (like this opening one) which
reflect responses not shared by the protagonist, as well as
ones which, while ostensibly from her viewpoint, manage
to reach beyond it. An example of this latter kind is the
paragraph beginning, "She had begun to teach school
from necessity," which not only reveals Marya's lack of
commitment as an educator, but justifies it by relating the
hardship of her work to that of "impecunious physicians,

doctors' assistants" who "don't even have the comfort of thinking that they are serving an ideal or the people, because their heads are always filled with thoughts of their daily bread, of firewood, of bad roads, of sickness." At the end of that paragraph, is it Marya herself, or the author, who refers to people like her as "stolid cart horses," and who says that "lively, alert, impressionable people who talk about their calling and about serving the ideal are soon weary of it and give up the work"? If this is not a judgment of Marya, at least it implies some lack of imagination or fire that may or may not be a consequence of her lot as rural teacher.

Without the coming of spring to her dormant soul— without the rebirth of childhood memories within her, however evanescent those memories may be—Marya's story would have little meaning for us except as social comment. If memory constitutes the self, the desires of memory the soul, Marya has neither—at least, not until that ecstatic vision at the railway crossing during which, blinded by light, she thinks she sees her mother and remembers her childhood. Until that moment, Marya is as faded as the photograph of her mother that she keeps in her schoolroom, a photograph in which nothing is left to be seen but "the hair and the eyebrows." Without memory, she has no will; her nature is wholly plastic and subservient to that of others, including the peasant driver of her cart. (If Joyce hadn't declared that he had read no Chekhov before writing *Dubliners,* I would have believed Marya to be one of the prototypes—Olenka of "The Darling" is another—for Maria in "Clay.")

The artfulness of "In the Cart" comes from Chekhov's use of a cart ride from a neighboring town to her home both to delineate Marya's selflessness—her lack of personal identity—and to prepare her, as well as the reader, for the moment at the crossing when happiness at last floods into her. What does this preparation consist of? First, she experiences, quite unexpectedly, a feeling of pity for Hanov, the friendly but rarely sober landowner whose carriage journey more or less parallels her own. The pity follows terror at the thought of his alcoholism. We make some connections between the pair, for both are, in their own way, ineffectual; but Marya quickly dismisses the thought that if she were his sister or his wife—a nurturing presence, not a sexual mate—she might yet save him from his downward plunge. ("Life is so arranged," she thinks, accepting her fate, that intimacy and "equal footing" with Hanov are absurd fancies.) Then, in the warm teahouse where she and Semyon, her driver, stop, Semyon warns a drunken peasant to stop his profanities since a "young lady," Marya herself, is there. The peasant apologizes. She enjoys her tea, and listens to the sound of an unseen accordion (a precursor to the memory of the sound of the piano that will come to her, one of the memories from childhood to be released in her moment of vision; Chekhov is always adept in his handling of such evocative, offstage sounds). Marya's plastic selflessness, like that of Joyce's Maria, arouses a kind of self-indulgence— a belief in their own virtue, perhaps—in others; one of the peasants recognizes her as the "school-ma'am from Vyazyvye. I know; she's a good sort." Another declares,

"She's all right!" And, on their way out of the teahouse, all of the peasants, whether drunk or sober, file past her, to shake her hand.

Her cart halts before the crossing barrier, for a train is about to pass. Here Marya, caught by the resemblance of a passenger to her mother, has the vision that not only re-captures her mother's precise image but so fully transports Marya herself back in time that she is again a child with secure feelings about herself and her family. Hanov's car-riage has come up to the crossing, too, "and seeing him she imagined such happiness as had never been, and smiled and nodded to him as an equal and an intimate." But Semyon cries an order to her as the barrier is lifted; Marya, at the story's end, is returned to the reality of her present condition.

Chekhov, as "unbiased witness," doesn't tell us what to make of such a story; in the letter to Suvorin mentioned at the beginning of this essay, he says "it is the jurors, that is, the readers, who must evaluate" any fictional account. Though Chekhov doesn't say so, the reader assumes the contrast between memory and reality to be extraordinar-ily painful to Marya; but perhaps even a memory as strong as this one will ebb, returning her to dormancy, numbness of soul. For a moment, though, she has come to life be-fore us as a human being, one as deluded by hope and de-sire as any of us.

No critical theory that I know of helps me in reading either this story or the corpus of which it is a part. "In the Cart" tells me of social indifference—social injustice—and of the diminishment of a woman's identity, but to approach it through any ideology (Marxist or feminist) misleads, for reasons that Virginia Woolf's statement makes clear. To be adequate to this little story, a theory would have to be concerned with human memory, and be broad enough to cover both the writer and his readers. It would need to demonstrate the relationship of memory to the values we consciously or subconsciously hold and to our comic absurdities as well as to our deepest and most buried feelings. It would be a theory that is not reductive, not psychoanalytical in the current sense, and it would apply beyond the boundaries of any specific culture. No doubt, that theory would acknowledge the hold a now-lost natural world still maintains on the psyche, and would connect that hold with the desire for freedom existing within us all. (Jung would be of greater help to it than Freud.) Without such a theory, we must depend—as we should in any case—upon pertinent biographical data (something that space limitations preclude from the present essay), the relationship of the story to the rest of the work, the insights of people we respect, and (most importantly) our own memories and the manner in which they direct or control our own responses. But such a theory is as unobtainable as the pure happiness of a limitless freedom.

7 The Moral Backbone
of *The Anatomy of Memory*

Though it took some persuasion on the part of an editor at Oxford University Press, I agreed about ten years ago to assemble an anthology about memory. I was then almost seventy, about to become an emeritus professor, and close to the completion of the third and final volume of *Court of Memory*, an autobiographical account that I had begun during the early days of the Cold War as a means of expressing and communicating the values and meanings of ordinary life. My initial hesitation to undertake the anthology had nothing to do with the pressures of work, or of deadlines of any sort; rather, it was the consequence of the importance of the subject to me. I have been called a memoirist, but I don't think of myself as one. I became an autobiographical writer primarily because on one long-ago winter night I underwent a kind of conversion. As humans, we are normally so unaware—so flawed by habitual sight—that it takes the likelihood of imminent loss to make us conscious of the profound value of all that surrounds us. I don't remember what particular crisis existed that night, but nuclear annihilation was such a possibility that the living world suddenly became sacramental to me, its parts interconnected.

Such an inner experience is really beyond language, but still it gave me, at long last, a voice—a way, that is, of interpreting and organizing experience. Why should the world have suddenly become holy? Not just because our species seemed about to destroy itself, I think. Something else—was it in my genetic memory, in my very body, or was it a response from my childhood?—had contributed to that awareness. I can't relive that ephemeral moment, but I've had others enough like it to bring its recall and to reinforce my sense of the value underlying the ordinary and commonplace. Personal memory, that subjective interpretation of experience, is the key to identity and consciousness, and yet it works in ways beyond conscious control: at almost every instant in our lives, it is effortlessly connecting the present with the past, finding likenesses and analogies and emotional associations in its continual attempts at understanding. Liable as it is to error and distortion, memory seems always in search of a synthesis, or unity, beyond its normal power. Our tragedy, as a species, may also lie in our genetic heritage; for through fright or phobia or some nationalistic or ethnic disease, we are apt to stop memory's search too soon by excluding others, by finding connections only in our own tight little group.

Memory is a vast subject, one that has been explored by theologians, philosophers, psychologists, and increasingly in our own time by neurobiologists; but what really matters most to me is its spiritual dimension, as the source of the desires that define the human soul. I wanted my anthology—

if indeed I agreed to undertake such an ambitious task—to explore the most crucial values and meanings that humans have, but I wanted to do that honestly, without sentimentality, facing up to all the suffering and tragedy and random acts of fate that beset us. I agreed to the undertaking when I remembered Augustine's *Confessions,* and indeed used sections of it at the beginning and the very end. But important as Augustine was to my subject and structure, I needed something else, preferably a testimony by a contemporary, and I found it in an essay by Andre Dubus.

I had been following the work of Andre Dubus for some years, for he too was a writer who valued memory and the spiritual quality of ordinary experience; as Tobias Wolff remarks in his fine introduction to Dubus's *Broken Vessels,* a collection of autobiographical essays, Dubus has "an unapologetically sacramental vision of life in which ordinary things participate in the miraculous, the miraculous in ordinary things."

In one of the essays in that book, the marvelous "Under the Lights," Dubus gives the account of his childhood experiences as a ball boy for the Lafayette, Louisiana, baseball team in which the crucial event is a home run hit by the most unlikely power hitter on the roster: "We never saw the ball start its descent, its downward arc to earth. For me, it never has. It is rising white over the lights high above the right field fence, a bright and vanishing sphere of human possibility soaring into the darkness beyond our vision." As is true of nearly all essays affirming the value of memory, this essay was written in retrospect, decades after the event; but the essay that comes at the end of the collection is a rare example of a memory not yet given the grace of time's passage: rather, it shows memory at work on tragic concerns of the present and the immediate past—at work, that is, when the help it can bring is almost indistinguishable from anguish, when "human possibility" would seem the remotest of hopes.

That essay, which gives the collection its title, was written at various intervals during Dubus's physical as well as spiritual struggle to recuperate from the accident which left him a cripple, dependent upon a wheelchair for the rest of his life, led to the dissolution of his marriage, and cost him the loss of the major custody of his children. Its details are too well known for me to recount them here. The essay is written as if the accident, and all that followed from it, exists in a continuum, and its composition is an obvious attempt to resist the impulse to die. At the close of the essay, that wish for death has been overcome for some months—by those who have helped him (friends, therapists, doctors, his children), by faith in God (despite, Dubus says in an address to the latter, the "sometimes incomprehensible, sometimes seemingly lethal way that You give"), by a human truth confirmed in literature, and by responses he first gained during his Marine Corps training.

Despite its length (it is far and away the longest essay I chose), I included "Broken Vessels" in my anthology, which was published in 1996 under the title of *The Anatomy of Memory*. Dubus's contribution is the moral backbone of that anatomy, the stiffening this particular book required—and the stiffening that all of us have need of, if we are to keep hope and human possibility alive within the atmosphere of the imperiled but shining little globe that is our home.

8 Reality and Imagination
in Literature and Psychology

This essay was written for a conference on Social Remembering held in 1998, which explored memory as a possible bridge connecting the various disciplines in the humanities. Participants were asked to respond to the presentation of a participant in another field, connecting those responses to their personal research or writing as well as to the current nature of the disciplines they represented. My essay is a response to the presentation of Marcia Johnson, a cognitive psychologist at Princeton, and it begins with a return to a long-ago moment whose crucial influence upon me is obvious from its mention in other, and quite different, essays.

Personal memory has been my chief resource as a writer ever since one wintry night in Ithaca, New York, about forty years ago. I've read that a conversion experience is common among autobiographical writers, and I don't think it too fanciful to say that such an experience happened to me that night. It was early in the Cold War; both Russia and the United States possessed nuclear weapons, and it seemed likely that one or the other, if not both, might end civilization, at least as we'd come to know it. I won't go into the details that marked that alteration in me, except to say that in looking out the window of my darkened study at a landscape illuminated only by starlight on the snow, I saw a mound of snow on a bird's nest in the backyard maple and knew, in a way I never had before, the value of everything I had pretty much taken for granted: everything in the phenomenal world, including that long-deserted bird's nest, was interconnected and sacred.

This was a subjective evaluation, and surely others have felt something like it in those moments when life is in precarious balance; but how had I come to know it? I can only conjecture that memory supplied the revelation; what I do know is that at once my memory was filled with supporting images from the past, most of which in other contexts would have seemed quite ordinary, as well as emotions toward them that told me how valuable they were. Without thought of publication, simply for my own self, I began that night the account that was to be the beginning of a lifetime of concern with personal memory, and which ultimately resulted in one book (or three, dependent upon how one looks at it), *Crossroads* (1968); *Court of Memory* (1986), which includes the first book; and *Stories from My Life with the Other Animals* (1993). As autobiography, it's fairly unusual (at least I know of no other quite like it) in that it was written not from one fixed present moment—I was not looking back upon a career or a life that was more or less completed—but from a whole series of them that began in my late thirties, each segment connecting the present moment with those elements of an ever-growing past that my memory associated with it. It gives for me the arc of human experience as I have lived it, but I would not—and most likely could not—have published it if I hadn't considered myself representational rather than unique.

Memory has been the thread linking everything I have written, whether novels or books about other authors or essays on topics distinct from myself. My growing insight into the workings of memory, from reading all sorts of imaginative literature as well as works by current neuroscientists and other specialists into the nature of the human mind, permitted me to be persuaded by an editor at Oxford University Press to edit an anthology, *The Anatomy of Memory* (1996), and twice to come out of retirement to offer a multidisciplinary course I devised, called "Mind and Memory: Explorations of Creativity in the Arts and Sciences." It is an undergraduate course, but a crucial component of it is a weekly series of public lectures by some of Cornell's most distinguished scientists and artists who speak of memory—collective as well as experiential—in connection with their own explorations and discoveries in science and art. Those lectures have attracted large audiences, in part because others—including colleagues—are interested in what scientists and artists are thinking as they go about their work; and also because they give an insight difficult to get elsewhere in these days of division and specialization into what lies at the very center, or heart, of what a university is or should be. In my mind the ideal undergraduate curriculum would include an introductory course into the nature and uses (as well as misuses) of memory as a foundation for everything else the students will learn.

Though I'm no longer connected with it, the course continues, now with a number of sections. During the two years that I offered it, the lecturers included three psychologists as well as a neurobiologist interested in the evolution of human behavior, a subject of interest to psychologists as well as many others. As luck would have it, Ulric Neisser, one of the founders of the field of cognitive psychology, gave his lecture just days before Marcia Johnson sent me some selected papers, the ones she intended to use as the basis for the presentation she has just given. Neisser spoke on "True and False Memories," so his subject was related to Marcia Johnson's. His emphasis was on the so-called "flashbulb memories," the ones occasioned by a crisis—Pearl Harbor, the assassination of John Kennedy, the *Challenger* explosion, the major earthquake in California that disrupted a World Series game. With the help of colleagues elsewhere in the country, he tested the memories of students, mainly freshmen, the day after the *Challenger* disaster, and the day after the earthquake, asking them to record such matters as where they were when they heard the news, what they said or did, and the reactions of others. Then he retested the same students three years later. These students still had vivid memories of details surrounding each event, but in the intervening years their imaginations had so abetted those memories, or later events had so altered them, that they were remembering details that never had happened, according to their earlier words. It occurred to me, in listening to Neisser, that my own experience of conversion—the moment in my darkened study in 1959 that told me that the phenomenal world was both sacred and interconnected (in other words, that a unity exists, however normally unavailable to our conscious minds)—was like a "flashbulb memory" in that it was precipitated by a crisis and that it was accompanied by a vivid recall of the environment in which it took place. The only differences were that for me the crisis had not actually occurred—it was simply imminent, a threat —and that the "flashbulb" that illuminated it was more metaphysical than real. It had transformed the world as it had transformed my life and determined not only my writing career but the direction of my teaching.

Among the papers that Marcia sent me was one called "Fact, Fantasy, and Public Policy" that fit my own inclinations, for it was informal, autobiographical, and sometimes quite funny. In it, she discusses—if not a "flashbulb"—a "lightbulb" of her own, the one that sent her off on her own professional path. (How do we distinguish "flashbulb" from "lightbulb" memories? Maybe the former apply to surprising or chaotic events external to us, the latter to revelations—insights or intuitions—that occur within. I would guess that my own revelation can be seen, according to such a distinction, more as a "lightbulb" than a "flashbulb.")

Marcia's lightbulb was occasioned by a drawing in an introductory psychology book of a figure, one ambiguous enough to be seen by some viewers as a duck, by others as a rabbit. It struck her that "the possibilities for experience were determined by the mind as well as the world." This view was compatible with the times, for she was at Berkeley during the chaotic and ambiguous sixties, but it leads to the frightening question that later she would ask: If even what we see depends on what we already know, and if what we remember depends on how we interpreted what we saw, and includes the not-necessarily-true inferences we drew, what then is the relationship of what we perceive and remember to reality? So a "lightbulb" determined Marcia's career, as an earlier one determined mine; she has been led by hers to examine the various kinds of "reality checks" that society at large and specific professions impose upon us, as well as those kinds of reality checks that can be used by each of us to determine whether a particular memory is based on experience—on perceptual evidence, inaccurate as it may be—or is wholly a product of our imagination or dreaming self. On the basis of their years of research and that of others—neuroscientists as well as psychologists investigating both normal and damaged minds—Marcia Johnson and her colleague Carol Raye have developed a source-monitoring framework. They describe it in terms understandable to an intelligent layperson; it seems eminently useful. But the difference in the nature of the lightbulbs that glowed for Marcia and for me suggests much about the difference in our separate journeys.

It is a simple truism that all of the creative arts impose imagination upon experience; but of those arts, only literature expresses imagination's value in words. Supposedly, the author's imagination reflects values that are meaningful to the rest of us. Does the subjectivity of our perceptions—which, as Marcia Johnson points out, are so capable of giving us misleading or untrue insights—have a redeeming feature, then? Let me phrase the question in a different way: Does imagination impart to what we see an intangible dimension that is a necessary part of our conception of reality? A good physical scientist would never answer "yes" to such a question. But as a writer, I would answer "yes": paradoxical as it may seem, the human world, and even the phenomenal world in which it is contained, would appear to me as devoid of meaningful substance were it not for my imposition of some quality upon what I perceive. I've had a number of later light-bulbs that depended on my first. One of them occurred in a moment of near-despair. It told me that my own sense of "reality," of whatever gives substance to human affairs, is a moral construction, requiring some possibility of goodness whatever our propensity toward greed, cruelty, and violence: without that human possibility, the world would seem phantasmagorical.

The question of the subjectivity of the arts—of the role that imagination plays—is such a vast one that I can't begin to discuss it adequately. I will limit myself to some comments about the two major movements in literature in the twentieth century. These tendencies—modernism and postmodernism—are also reflected in the other arts, and for that matter outside them. At about midpoint in the century, postmodernism appeared, soon supplanting modernism in significance. At least, that is the prevalent view of those who place labels on the products of human thought and imagination. In the most encompassing sense, limited only by its reference to Western civilization, modernism is applied to the growing emphasis on the individual, to the movement which replaced medievalism many hundreds of years ago; much of postmodern theory, as I will soon indicate, contradicts such an emphasis. In literature itself, though, modernism is usually used to characterize that kind of writing in the late nineteenth and twentieth centuries which distinguished itself from both naturalism and realism. In our century, modernism and postmodernism refer to literary positions that have much in common, including a dissatisfaction with conventional forms. Individual writers of our own postmodern day, including some very good ones, frequently reflect both modernist and postmodernist attitudes, just as earlier writers like Nathanael West foreshadow postmodernism itself. (For that matter, so does *Don Quixote,* written by Cervantes in the early years of the seventeenth century!) All of us exist in a flux, a continuum. For the purpose of this talk, I've been looking at the various and sometimes ambiguous and often conflicting definitions given to these terms, as they apply to literature. I know that a clearer distinction separates them than their definitions imply, and so will attempt to rise above the flux far enough to indicate what I can see.

What I see are two competing interpretations of reality, one inner and the other outer. The first—modernism —goes inward, for it is alienated by the material considerations of the exterior world; it goes inward in pursuit of spiritual essences, of enduring values that transcend the randomness, the apparent pointlessness, of daily existence. The latter—postmodernism—goes outward, frequently delighting in the immense variety, the very randomness and irrationality that modernism attempts to surmount. Nothing—certainly nothing so precious (in either sense of the word) as a spiritual essence—can be said to define or bind us. But in a way "nothing" itself can be said to represent us, for "nothing" is the end not only of our individual lives but of the civilization of which we are part. (Look further into the future and the earth melts into the expanding and dying sun.) To the degree that "modern," at least in its conventional usage, refers to the present— that is, to a moment in time always to be replaced by another present—"postmodern" has a certain foreboding quality about it, as if survivors of the modern period were simply going through the motions, the human game being in some ultimate sense already over: in this respect, postmodern literature often is suffused with an apocalyptic atmosphere. Actually, the notion of life as a game is congenial to the postmodern mind, and given its assumptions, its literature is surprisingly playful and self-referential. Given those assumptions, though, postmodernism is deterministic, the characters in its novels mere chess pieces, or puppets in a show, their movements dictated by an intellectual construct, a grand metaphor imagined by their maker.

To illustrate the difference separating the two movements, let me refer to Marcel Proust, an early literary modernist. Memory is Proust's subject, far more than is the case for most writers. According to him, "The true paradises are the paradises we have lost." Why is this so?

He classifies memory into two types. One is conscious recall, the kind we can will into existence. It provides something like a photograph of a past image, something fixed in time. The kind he values consists of involuntary memories—brought before us by a smell, a musical phrase, or even something so trivial as a momentary loss of one's balance. These carry us back to an earlier episode, evoking all the emotions surrounding that episode so that we relive it. But involuntary memories can transcend time and put us in touch with the eternal "essence of things" that we were unaware of during our initial experience; imagination intertwined with the return of the actual event makes the involuntary memory superior to the event itself, and this is the reason that "true paradises" are those "we have lost."

Virginia Woolf provides another example of modernism. In a famous or infamous remark, she declared, "On or about December, 1910, human character changed." What she meant, of course, was that *she* had changed, in her perception of reality and hence in her attitude toward the fictional characters she and others created. In trying to make sense of this odd remark, critics sometimes attribute it to a lightbulb that turned on in her head—lightbulbs seem to be part of my theme—as the consequence of viewing a highly controversial exhibition of Post-Impressionist paintings assembled in London by her friend Roger Frye. The change told her that "reality" was not to be found in our social structures, our business or industrial activities, our wars and competing ideologies, but rather in our inner life or stream of consciousness, particularly in our moments of "being"—moments in which we are most intensely alive, most responsive to "a token of some real thing beyond appearances" that later can make us perceive a transcendent pattern in existence.

Now it is obvious from what I've said about that star-filled night in 1959 that I must belong to the modernist camp. The insight that came to me was involuntary; if it is an example of Proust's involuntary memory, its particular antecedent is unknown to me. But let me be just as outrageous as Virginia Woolf and say that the change from modernism to postmodernism occurred on the same night in 1959 that I saw the mounded snow on a bird's nest, and a lightbulb switched on in my head. For what had influenced me—not only the imminent threat of nuclear annihilation, but the knowledge of Buchenwald and Auschwitz and other irrational and dehumanizing horrors of our century, horrors resonating against much of the unsettling information humans have learned about themselves through and since Darwin and Freud—surely had influenced others: in literature, something called "black humor" had already arrived, and black humor presaged postmodernism. A grim determinism was surely in the frigid air during those dark hours. I am bolstered in what I'm saying about the birth of postmodernism that very night because the highly talented Thomas Pynchon was probably writing away then, in another Ithaca room. His novel *V,* an early postmodern work, would appear a few years later; and Tom was an undergraduate advisee of mine who never required advice.

So I certainly understand the reasons for postmodernism, and recognize that postmodernist writers like Pynchon have produced some of the most influential novels of the past four decades. I share with them the sense that the conventions of storytelling are more outmoded than even Proust and Woolf felt them to be. Why didn't I have another kind of conversion experience, then, one that would have headed me down the postmodernist route? Because I was already too old for that. Because I was married and the father of two young sons. Because I lacked the required inventive facility. Because I was what I was. To write from the self—wholly from one's memories— has enormous limitations for a creative writer, for it excludes the invention of fictional characters or events; but it has benefits I found equally immense. What a difference it makes, to turn either inward or outward! Turn inward and your reality can still be invested with a spiritual truth. Turn inward and you realize that neither you nor the actual people memory brings to mind are puppets: you and they remain capable of free will, each person determining, within necessary and ultimately tragic limits, his or her unique destiny. For here your memory is working to understand the present in terms of your past, through all the associations the past makes with it; though the future is ever in your mind, you bring to the present the rich potential you have discovered only in that past. Will your discoveries influence others, and can they have a cumulative social effect? Conceivably, this just might be the case —that is, if you write of them as honestly and clearly as you can in the expectation that others will see in your experiences a reflection of their own. These were the thoughts that came to me in the weeks and months following that crucial night, for I hoped I could help bring about a change.

The determinism found in postmodern novels predates the coming of theorists—postmodernists themselves—to our universities. Their early pronouncements, indicating the writer's entrapment in the social and linguistic texts, are equally deterministic. Most of that determinism still hangs on, as Jonathan Culler demonstrates in *Literary Theory: A Very Short Introduction,* a concise, balanced, and remarkably lucid guide to the maze of theory. In expanding on some remarks by Michel Foucault about the "decentering of the subject" brought about by psychoanalysis, linguistics, and anthropology, Culler says:

> If the possibilities of thought and action are determined by a series of systems which the subject does not control or even understand, then the subject is 'decentered' in the sense that it is not a source or centre to which one refers to explain events. It is something formed by these forces. Thus, psychoanalysis treats the subject not as a unique essence but as the product of intersecting psychic, sexual, and linguistic mechanisms. Marxist theory sees the subject as determined by class position: it either profits from others' labour or labours for others' profit. Feminist theory stresses the impact of socially constructed gender roles on making the subject what he or she is. Queer theory has argued that the heterosexual subject is constructed through the repression of the possibility of homosexuality.

Neuroscientists believe that their research into the human brain has overthrown the determinism that has haunted us since Descartes, who saw the mind as separate from the brain. But now we know that the mind is not divorced from the brain, or from the material world. We know also that memory is the key to consciousness, and human consciousness constructs memories—as Antonio Damasio has remarked—of the possible future as well as of the past. To Gerald Edelman, the mind (in its historical development, and at each and every moment for the living individual) is a biological process, a process that demonstrates an intentionality not found elsewhere in nature; because of its awareness of time, it possesses "the ability to model the past and the future." Thus our minds permit us enough free will to make present changes, enabling us to alter the future in significant ways. We have suffered far too long a sense of our "decentration," Edelman says, almost as if he were responding to the above quotation; neuroscience demonstrates that fatalism, like all forms of "silly reductionism," does not apply.

In the form of postmodernism, though, determinism —as I hope I have shown—still haunts our thinking. And surely all of us, postmodernists or not, have felt the hold of external events upon us—particularly those events that make the reading of twentieth-century history such a painful exercise. Compared to the glow briefly over Hiroshima or the illumination over fire-bombed Dresden, or over much more recent cities and villages with their straw roofs in flames, doesn't my little lightbulb in 1959 seem dreadfully dim? I tell myself that mine is quite different in kind, and cannot be compared; that individually, personally, we all carry in memory a similar bulb, and that if all these bulbs were extinguished, we'd be huddled together in the hallucinatory dark. How do we regain greater control over the external world, making our institutions a

Reality and Imagination in Literature and Psychology

better representation of what we know to be true within us? E. M. Forster, an uneasy modernist, foresaw the dangers of the split as early as 1910 and said, "Only connect." But how? A major irony of postmodernist theory is that, while it is quite adept at illustrating the blindnesses, prejudices, and ambiguities in a given culture's text, any necessary social change requires in us what theory denies that we possess: free will and an encompassing spiritual insight.

Postmodernist theorists could say that the modernists I have cited represent only the cultural elite, and that my own views about human will and spiritual essence illustrate no more than my own privileged condition as a member both of the white majority and the professional class. I can reply that they too are elitist—actually, even more than I am—and furthermore that the spiritual revelation that came to me so long ago may well have been a biological memory from the distant past, from the primitive ancestors I share with them. (This kind of genetic determinism I gladly accept.) I can also say that the irony implicit in theory represents the contradiction between theory and the theorists' own essence or spiritual nature. And I can add that countless individuals in the past have battled all the powers assembled against them for the sake of their personal insights—and that many of these individuals have made a small difference, and a few have even won.

Ultimately, determinism rules, in accordance with physical laws; nothing I've said really contradicts that. But life—conscious life—remains a mystery in which we muddle along, doing the best we can to discover the truths that can guide us. Given the deceptions, the half-truths and outright lies we find in the media as well as in Washington and other centers of political and economic power today, we desperately need the kind of insight that the research of psychologists like Marcia Johnson provides us; for today more than ever we need to be aware of the possibilities of error in our own memories and in what others tell us is true. We need to devise "reality checks." Can we, as readers, also impose a "reality check" on any given writer's imagination that is based on the qualities of imagination itself? The question may seem quixotic, but as a writer and reader I'm always doing precisely that. Memory makes associations; it imposes whatever order it can on experience in the attempt to make sense of it. To my way of thinking, it is searching always for a synthesis or unity beyond its grasp: memory itself has a spiritual dimension that we refer to as the soul. To the degree that another person's imagination is devoted to that search—devoted with integrity, without sentimentality of any kind—I give it my measure of validity.

9 Ubiquitous Augustine

For ten years, I taught an undergraduate Cornell course, "The Modern European Novel"—a course made famous through the published lectures prepared for it by one of its former teachers, Vladimir Nabokov. The novels I chose were seldom the same as his. Though over the years I changed some of my texts, the one that opened the course remained the same. Augustine's Confessions *is anything but modern; it is not a novel; and its author was born in Africa. Still, its influence on later literature is so pronounced that Augustine's spiritual autobiography became a major point of reference for my students and me throughout the term.*

Its influence, of course, extends beyond Europe to America. That the Confessions *continues to provide a point of reference for American writers—novelists and critics among them—is obvious from this essay, concerned with four books published in recent years:* E. L. Doctorow's City of God, *Jonathan Bishop's* In Time, *Garry Wills's* Saint Augustine, *and James Olney's* Memory & Narrative: The Weave of Life-Writing. *It's possible that I am alone in reading all four, Bishop's book in particular never having been intended for a wide audience; but "Ubiquitous Augustine" presupposes no advance knowledge of any of them. Taken together, though, they provide at least a partial way of viewing the human place in the cosmos, from Augustine's day to the present.*

The Spring 2000 issue of the *Virginia Quarterly Review* contains an essay by John S. Spong, "Christ and the Body of Christ: Is There a Future for the Christian Church?" that says the theistic God of Christianity has become un-believable, its myths rendered inoperative by the knowl-edge that the Earth we inhabit is a tiny planet circling a sun that is itself but one star in a galaxy of a billion stars, our galaxy but one of at least 125 billion more. How can we continue to hold to "the assumption that in the Christ figure the theistic God from beyond the sky has entered human history and has been encountered in human form" to save us from our sins by sacrificing Himself to appease that God? Humans were never "perfect" before their descent into sin; in the post Darwinian world we in-habit, we realize that human beings, like other forms of life, reflect the evolutionary struggle for survival, and re-main "unfinished, still evolving, emerging creatures."

Nothing remarkable attaches itself to this contempo-rary rejection of Christian doctrine; after all, we are the heirs of Copernicus and Kepler and Galileo, of Freud and Einstein as well as Darwin. Through optical instruments such as the Hubble Space Telescope and radio telescopes like the one in Puerto Rico operated by Cornell, we are reaching toward the edges of space and billions of years back toward the origins of the universe. In the latter half of the nineteenth century, long before Earth had become such an inconsequential dot in the cosmos, the investigations of Darwin and others had already led to rejections of a theistic deity. In the preceding two centuries, deists (who included some of this nation's founding fathers) thought God, having given a spin to the gears of His Creation, was thereafter content to let the mechanism run without further divine intervention. Spong's views are remarkable chiefly because of his continuing attachment to Christianity, for decades as an Episcopal priest and decades more as a bishop.

Both the Old Testament and the New Testament—including the Gospels—are, he says, interpretive human explanations, as are the historic creeds of the church:

> There are no words, no traditions, and no theological formulas that are not explanations, and every explanation is time-limited, and its "truth" is time-bound. Theism, we need to understand, is but another explanation of a God experience. The death of an explanation does not require the denial of the experience. So all of these symbols of our faith story—our Bible, our creeds, our doctrines, our sacred traditions—can be and must be debated, compromised, changed and even surrendered if necessary. Only the experience of God is eternal and that experience ultimately has no words.

Spong, now Bishop of Newark emeritus and currently a lecturer at Harvard, remains a Christian; for God "is real for me, a mystical, undefinable presence that I can experience but never explain," while Jesus "is the revelation of this God for me, not because of miracle stories or excessive pre-modern claims, but because he is portrayed as one who is fully alive with the life of God . . ." In the tradition of Luther, Spong has posted on the Internet "Twelve Theses" in keeping with this essay and with a book he has written, *Why Christianity Must Change or Die.*

I came across Spong's essay so closely after I had finished E. L. Doctorow's *City of God* that it seemed a small miracle—a paradox, as miracles are—wrought for my sake alone by the God who no longer keeps watch over me or the sparrows that fall. For Doctorow's new novel, its title an echo of a book by Saint Augustine, not only takes on the issues raised by the Right Reverend Spong but seems to have used him (the evidence is in a brief reference to the unusually liberal nature of the Episcopalian diocese of Newark) as a model for the construction of his fictional character Thomas Pemberton, rector of a small Episcopalian church in Manhattan. Like Spong, Pemberton has lost his belief in the divinity of Jesus as well as in the Old Testament accounts that prepared the way for Him; nevertheless—again like Spong—Pemberton maintains the belief in God. In one sense, Pemberton is the more radical of the two, in wanting to jettison Christ entirely while holding on to the ethical tenets of Christianity; in another sense, he may be less so, for he is still willing to accept signs of a mysterious intervention in human affairs. (Such a responsiveness to signs is necessary to the plot, for after all this is a novel, with all the strengths and weaknesses of that literary form; but how am I to protest, given the providential arrival for me of the Spong essay?)

For a writer not only to devote a novel to religious matters but to suggest a way out of the contemporary

spiritual dilemma is, on the face of it, a remarkably coura-
geous undertaking, quite unlike anything Doctorow or
any other reputable novelist of our day has attempted.
What audacity, what chutzpah, to write a novel in which
an Episcopalian priest renounces not God but the Trinity,
and ends up a convert to Judaism! But this innovative new
branch of Judaism has lost its provincial nature and all of
the elaborations—the prophecies and no longer tenable
miracles—associated with Jews as the chosen people.

A reader who ignores the words on the dust jacket of
City of God will at first be bewildered by its juxtapositions
—its apparently fragmentary nature. We need those words
to understand that we're being exposed to the workbook
of a fictional New York City novelist who is recording
"the contents of his teeming brain" as he begins his search
to uncover the reason that "the large brass cross that hung
behind the altar of St. Timothy's, a run-down Episcopalian church in lower Manhattan" has vanished, to reap-
pear, mysteriously, "on the roof of the Synagogue for
Evolutionary Judaism, on the Upper West Side."

Everett, the novelist, thinks that the mystery might
provide him the subject for his next novel, and from the
various ideas for subjects we find in his workbook, we can
assume he really needs something better—or at least
something less depressing—than the ones he has put
down. One reviewer of the book has suggested, rather
meanly, that Doctorow has simply tossed into it, along
with much else, all his own discarded fictional concepts;
but everything revealed by that "teeming brain" (including narrative poems of a biographical and autobiographi-

cal nature, explorations of the implications of popular songs, cameo appearances by Einstein and Wittgenstein as well as the now almost-forgotten Bishop Pike, a description of the Big Bang which created the expanding universe out of nothing, depictions of predatory practices on this bloody planet even by birds whose songs and feathers we admire, and the imaginative retelling of the gradual decimation of an actual Jewish ghetto in Lithuania during the Holocaust) become part of the postmodern world we all inhabit, shards demonstrating not only our lack of cohesion but the often extraordinary brutality humans inflict on each other that contributes to a pervasive sense of spiritual emptiness. A skeptic, Everett has been in pursuit of purely secular subjects for his novels; what he arrives at through his pursuit of the mystery behind the journey of the cross is a narrative of both sexual and spiritual love granted to his renegade Episcopalian priest and an attractive woman, recently widowed, who serves as the progressive rabbi of the Synagogue for Evolutionary Judaism.

In another novel, the transference of the cross from the altar of an Episcopalian church to the roof of a synagogue would be an intrusive, finger-pointing symbol, but in *City of God* it is a mysterious sign of God's presence, at least as it appears in—or to—our human consciousness. (That consciousness, given its origin in the cosmic dust that materialized after the explosion that created the still-expanding universe, is quite incredible in itself.) So Thomas Pemberton considers the journey of the cross as a sign; and it must be the premise on which the story turns, for no other explanation is offered. Like the actual Bishop Spong with his "Twelve Theses," Father Thomas Pemberton and the progressive Rabbi Sarah Blumenthal of this novel have discovered that our growing knowledge of the cosmos, and of human history and ourselves, requires the rejection from religion of whatever no longer applies, leaving each person with her or his individual experience of God, the communal nature of religion now being supported by whatever can be salvaged from tradition.

Why is it that I find myself in agreement with all three of them and yet feel—especially in the novel—a touching naiveté in the resolutions that all three have come to? (While prevalent elsewhere in the novel, irony seems absent here.) I agree with Sarah Blumenthal in her discussion of the human soul at one of the Friday night services at the synagogue when she says that the "beautiful" word *soul* "carries so much, it expresses, really, longing for union with God, for the final resolution of all our questioning . . . ," for my own feelings and experiences have led me to think of the soul as a quality, as a desire for unity carried perhaps in our experiential as well as our biological memories, a hope for an ultimate synthesis that underlies the differing quests of science and art but that consciousness itself, however much it tries, keeps us from achieving. And from the time I first began to think about such concerns, it struck me that religion always has been the institutionalization of a pre-existent spiritual impulse within each of us: the institutional development of rituals and a particular history (usually replete with miracles) in order to explain and to give social and political direction to what, as Spong says, is a personal and wordless experience. We are social creatures, so what else could we expect? Bishop Spong and the two redemptive figures in Doctorow's novel are seeking, for our salvation, a spiritual regeneration through institutional means. But if they won the congregations they require, how long would the purity and idealism of their conceptions last before the inevitable elaboration and distortion of them? To put it another way, the Society of Friends and the Unitarians already occupy much of their ground, and have yet to redeem the world.

Jonathan Bishop's *In Time*—a title to be taken in two ways at once, secular and spiritual—can be seen as a serious effort to extricate Christianity from such problems, and—like Everett's workbook—is a receptacle into which Bishop can put the contents of his thoughts; but "Everett" is fictional, or maybe quasi-fictional, while "Bishop" has to be the construction that the reader makes of the actual person whose work he or she is reading.

The brief "Preface" which proceeds Bishop's "Introduction" serves the same clarifying function that the dust jacket of Doctorow's novel does: it tell us that his is primarily a philosophical approach—though one with a literary emphasis and with supporting elements from personal experience—to the interrelated questions of time, metaphor, and identity. The middle term (only later is this made explicit) refers to the imaginative faculty that must underlie all such philosophical inquiry. So here we have an interconnected triad, one in which metaphor is the necessary link between time and identity. Is this triad intended to remind us of the Trinity? It turns out that yes, it should; but in this preface the religious implications are withheld. Gradually, the reader who stays the course perceives the approximation of Bishop's triad—really a metaphor in itself—to God, Christ, and temporal human identity.

Bishop's book is divided into sections of time, moving from "Now" (or the present) to "Then" (the past in the present) to "Once" (origins) and then to "When" (whatever the future contains). The introduction and first two sections permit the entrance of personal and historical memory, with an acknowledgment of losses and of what continues, as well as a discussion of pertinent literary and other texts. The details of his personal life, including his teaching career, that Bishop gives us are, while controlled, moving; and his literary insights—into figures like Emerson, Thoreau, and T. S. Eliot, for example—are persuasive. One can be engrossed in his text even by the amount of vexation he can give—at least to a reader like me—both for his acceptance of the philosophical dualism of Descartes and his ready rejection of widely admired figures such as Augustine and Proust. (I assume such provocation is intentional.)

The first half of *In Time* is a preparation for the last half, which primarily is a study of passages in both the Old and New Testaments (an investigation not intended for the casual reader). Bishop's frequent use of one word —eschatology, dealing as it does with the circling found in the doctrine of Christ's death, resurrection, and eventual return—suggests much about his view of time and reflects the circling within his text. Beginnings prefigure ends, but temporal creatures that we are, both elude us;

and no historical moment contains the fullness of time. In our own lives, as in a larger history, certain rhythms are to be found—variations upon a theme, never a simple repetition. Does the past contain a prophecy of the present, the present of the future? It is Judaic-Christian history that matters to Bishop in answering such a question. The Old Testament prophets foresaw the coming of a new Messiah. Jesus, as historical figure, was influenced by such prophecies, including that of a new Promised Land, and by the ritualistic sacrifices. But Jesus, at the Last Supper and in the sacrifice of himself for us (and it is notable that Bishop avoids capitalizing Jesus' pronoun), translates the past into self-sacrifice and an encompassing love, and it is this that is celebrated in the Eucharist, as the participants acknowledge their oneness in him and the promise to be revealed in the fullness of time.

Though Bishop's explorations into the Bible offer some interpretations that strike me—one admittedly not an adept in this field—as wholly original, his conclusions are clearly within the tradition to which he subscribes. He differs from many others, though, in his scrupulous treatment of Jesus and the Old Testament scribes as historical figures, each caught in a particular movement of time. Like those scribes, Jesus speaks in parables, and does nothing "literally." He "does not write—unless ironically, in the dust." It can't be otherwise, for historically, Jesus—like those scribes and like us today—exists in a given moment of time, and writing only restores us to that moment, to whatever is apparently true there and then.

"Time," Bishop says, "is an ambiguous gift of God; who is always ahead of us, not behind." We can perceive

His "gift" only metaphorically. Jesus "is a parable"; he is "one we don't outlive: he is in front of us still." He is a "sign"—in Biblical history, the ultimate prophet, subsuming his predecessors.

What separates Spong from Bishop? Aren't both speaking of an experience that time-bound words cannot encompass? Treated metaphorically, are the Old and New Testaments a valid approach to the fullness of time, or are they simply a human explanation? To Bishop, the Bible is, I assume, both; Jesus, the poet who writes no words, gives us the metaphors we need to find ourselves.

Each of the recent books here under review at least mentions Augustine, who is, after all, a seminal figure in discussions of spiritual as well as literary concerns. Everett, the writer of Doctorow's novel, admires Augustine for his use of language, for his "voice." To Pemberton, the priest already doubting the framework of his faith, Augustine is no more than that, simply a rhetorician. Here Bishop and Pemberton are in agreement, for Bishop finds Augustine a fluent theological politician caught up in the conflicting dogmas of his age. What came of Augustine's famous conversion in the garden—his conversion to Catholicism upon hearing a little girl say a few words? It brought him no new comprehension of God, for God remained for him a Neoplatonic conception, Augustine continuing to be entrapped in the conceptual abstractions of eternal time.

Garry Wills takes a contrary opinion. I find it refreshing to look at Augustine through the research of this polyglot scholar. Wills disguises the scholarship that went into the making of his *Saint Augustine;* as consequence, his book is as lucid as it is brief, and can be recommended as a biography to any reader curious about the historical figure of the man who, in Wills's words, was "the creator of the theology that would resound" in the Catholic Church—and whose continuing influence can still be felt in psychology and literature and in all our explorations of memory.

Wills gently corrects what he finds to be the many misapprehensions that have distorted our apprehension of Augustine. For example, the title of his most famous book —known to us as his *Confessions*—should more properly be translated, Wills instructs us, as his *Testimony,* since Augustine "sincerely experienced his memories as drenched in God's grace," his words a testimony to that. The Latin *confessio* covers far more than a private admission of sins, but it doesn't imply the public revelations of intimate secrets so prevalent in present-day memoirs. Augustine's writings reflect a process in the mind of a man whom Wills describes as a "tireless seeker":

> Impatient with all preceding formulas, even his own, he was drawn and baffled by mystery. We seek one mystery, God, with another mystery, ourselves. We are mysterious to ourselves because of God's mystery in us: "Our mind cannot be understood, even by itself, because it is made in God's image."

In the current neurobiological view, the "mind" is created by the brain, but—unlike the brain—it is clearly not a substance but a quality. Though Wills does not mention this, the *Testimony* describes Augustine's long labor before his own reason made it clear to him that God is not a substance existing everywhere and at every moment in the observable universe of space and time. God, then, is Mind. However circumscribed or otherwise limited it is, the human mind is an image of the Divine Mind, containing more than it can know it knows.

Augustine valued the community of others for the help its members could mutually provide in the pursuit of such a mystery. He moved from one communal group to another, conversation being a sharing of intellectual discovery. His own love of language led him to rhymes, puns, and sometimes pyrotechnical displays, but despite such rhetorical excess—and indeed Wills calls him an "antirhetorical rhetorician"—he had a lifelong abhorrence of lies. To him, all lying was sinful; but lying about one's religious beliefs was blasphemous, a sin to be avoided, whatever the political risk. Though Plotinus had been an influence upon him, Augustine's conversion to Catholicism was authentic. Augustine depicts his personal struggle before conversion as the conflict within his own divided will. His introduction of will—and his depiction of a will in opposition to itself—into the terms of theology is Augustine's major contribution to that field, as later it would be to the fields of philosophy and psychology. Wills suggests that if we read the *Testimony* properly, we see that Augustine's memories of his conversion and of all the earlier events of his life are viewed from a later perspective. The final three books of the work, Wills observes, represent the three parts of Augustine's thinking as he considers his past: "the human mind's mystery, God's creation of time out of eternity, and God's triume nature." Recognizing this, a reader can see the application of these three concerns to Augustine's reconstruction of his earlier self, for that reconstruction acts out his own discovery that present memory always informs the past.

But if the present informs and even interprets the past, what is now the present will in itself be interpreted when it becomes part of the past. If memory is integral to identity, the sense of self, then must not that sense (constituting the ever-moving present as contained in the past) be amorphous, always in flux? The self, in contemplating itself, can get entangled in questions like that, and so must find its definition in narrative. For the self can never know itself except in relationship to the story of its past and all that surrounds that past—or so James Olney persuasively demonstrates in *Memory & Narrative: The Weave of Life-Writing.*

His book is no less than a history of writing about the self—he prefers the term "life-writing," even though he's not wholly content with it, to "autobiography" or the obviously inadequate "memoir." He limits his scope only in that his references are to writers in the Western world; to provide a necessary focus, he gives primary attention to three—Augustine, Jean-Jacques Rousseau, and Samuel Beckett—to represent the beginning, the middle, and the end (the present end: the narrative of our self-narratives is, of course, a never-ending one).

Had Olney ignored all other writers to concentrate on his representative figures (something, given his theory of narrative, he can't and won't do), his field would still have been formidable; for as a treatment of self-narratives, it must encompass the entirety of the life-writings of the individuals under study—the major works, that is, of Augustine, Rousseau, and Beckett. A more ambitious task is difficult to envision, and Olney refers to it as "exploratory." Despite the extent of material to be covered, however, his explorations are carried out in a prose that is free from jargon; and—while his patient accumulation and elucidation of details may on occasion strain the reader's own patience—the style is everywhere a model of clarity.

His consideration of Augustine amplifies what Wills summarizes. Olney's description of Augustine's conception of the mind is of assistance to the reader: As an image, however imperfect, of God, the mind is a triad, being composed of memory, understanding, and will; they are as interconnected as the Trinity they reflect, the first of the Father, the second of the Son, and the third of the Holy Ghost. God exists within us as the source of our memory, and that presence is the reason we can never fully comprehend ourselves; the Son, in taking on our physical form, provides us with what understanding we have; and the Holy Ghost, informed by memory and understanding, becomes another name for love and charity—the qualities that can direct our present behavior and future actions through a willing acceptance. (In thinking of this, I at once saw Freud's own triad of id, ego, and superego as a wholly secular emendation of Augustine's: was Freud ever aware of such an influence upon him?)

For Augustine, the self is far less consequential than the divine mystery beyond his present understanding; and that mystery, encompassing our own, is the subject of his search. In using Augustine's title for his own *Confessions,* Rousseau must have had the former in mind. Still, in turning only inward—in finding the contemplation of himself such a delightful and engrossing subject—Rousseau broke from the Augustinian tradition: it was under his warm self-gaze that Romanticism burst forth with its subjective flowering. My own reading of Rousseau's *Confessions* was such a disquieting experience that in my mind I turned it into the novel it almost is, a first-person account by an unreliable narrator as he moves from sensitive appreciation of his natural surroundings to an ever-deepening paranoia he never comprehends. Of course, to see how Rousseau transformed Augustine's love of God into what he hoped to be love of self—a goal that ended up hopelessly entangled with the self-love he thought he could avoid—one would need to read not just his *Confessions* but Rousseau's other work, especially the two other books in which he vainly attempted to depict his true self (the reading that Olney has done).

Though Beckett's fiction and plays have long been perceived as the projection through characters of his own inner life, he might seem at first an unlikely representative upon which to conclude the ongoing story of self-writing; but his choice turns out to be as inevitable as that of Rousseau in the center. Years ago, Olney was intrigued by Augustinian references in Beckett's work; it is now apparent to him how much the dual traditions of Augustine and Rousseau permeate Beckett's writing. Given all that he had absorbed from the past, given his situation in the twentieth century, Beckett couldn't have searched beyond the self for divine answers, even had he wanted to; and Rousseau had already demonstrated the impossibility of finding the self through the self. In short, given such an impasse, all Beckett could do was to take impossibility itself—the shapeless mess of the self—as his major subject. To paraphrase the constant paradox of his characters, he can't go on but must go on, somehow shaping that mess into art. Olney returns several times to a remark Beckett once made about himself: "I take no sides. I am interested in the shape of ideas. There is a wonderful sentence in Augustine: 'Do not despair; one of the thieves was saved. Do not presume: one of the thieves was damned.' That sentence has a wonderful shape. It is the shape that matters."

In summarizing what is most obvious about Olney's remarkable achievement, I find I've said very little about what his book really offers. Yes, shape matters, but shape is disclosed in narration, and Olney's own narration gives shape to the continual interweaving found in the history of life-writing, and in so doing offers us a way to consider ourselves. Maybe we can't go on, but as sentient beings moving in the flux of time toward an unknown destination, we must.

10 The River Runs Through Us

Those of us whose academic careers were determined by a love of literature nearly always have given our major attention to past and present writers whose reputations were already established. In recent decades, though, a wholly justifiable attempt has been made to add to this canon those writers who had been excluded from it by societal prejudice of their culture, skin color, sexual orientation, and other matters.

Only in the years since my retirement from Cornell have I become aware of the many writers in my area—and no doubt in other areas of the nation—who have long been ignored by teachers like me, since they exist outside of our classifications. Without affiliation to colleges and universities, they often form into groups that meet—much like a college writing workshop—to evaluate the work of their members. If such groups make any kind of discrimination in their membership (or so it seems to me, from the groups I have come to know), that discrimination is based only on talent and dedication; otherwise, they represent much of the variety that is America.

The River Runs Through Us

From my reading of the work produced by the groups I've par-
ticularly come to admire, I can say that the writers are aware of
injustice and other human shortcomings. And yet they—or at
least a majority of them—are neither political enough to be con-
sidered challenging nor young enough to be considered promising.
Often their concern is less to shock or outrage than it is to affirm
the qualities that give depth and consequence to life despite (and
even because of) its hardships, reversals, and eventual tragedy. Be-
ing relatively unknown—their work is not to be found in the
major anthologies—and of no interest to ideologists, they arouse
no academic interest, even though they speak of essential human
needs and desires. In making such large generalizations, which
may have more applicability to poets than to prose writers, I real-
ize I am describing qualities I've always hoped that my own
prose might imply.

Ann Silsbee was a fine poet who fits my description; she died
at the very moment her work was gaining the larger audience it
deserves.

Ann Silsbee, whose unexpected death on August 28
saddened all those who had come to know and admire
her over the decades of her life in Ithaca, possessed a variety of talents. She was a painter, pianist, and composer as
well as a poet, though poetry—or so I judge from the
artistry of the two books I've just read—must have become the dominant creative concern of her later years.

Only a few days before she died, I phoned Ann to say
that I had agreed to review *Orioling,* which had won the
2001 Benjamin Saltman Poetry Award. During our con-

versation, she told me that a second book of her poetry, *The Book of Ga,* was about to be published. At my suggestion, she mailed me a copy of the manuscript so that I could review them together. I am glad that I asked to see that second book. Ann had been pleased that the first publisher to consider *The Book of Ga* had accepted it at once; having read it, I can see the reason for such a quick and affirmative response.

Structurally, the two volumes are quite different. *Orioling* is a collection of separate poems, each complete in itself. Some of the poems in *The Book of Ga* can stand alone (ten of them were published in magazines, and one of them was nominated for a Pushcart Prize). Nevertheless, the book itself is one long poem, all of its parts interconnected through its story of a life as well as through the river that is both a physical fact and the channel within which that narrative flows.

In his later years, William Butler Yeats wrote what most critics consider his finest poetry, including "Sailing to Byzantium." "Once out of nature," Yeats writes as the concluding stanza for that poem,

> I shall never take
> My bodily form from any natural thing,
> But such a form as Grecian goldsmiths make
> Of hammered gold and gold enamelling
> To keep a drowsy Emperor awake;
> Or set upon a golden bough to sing
> To lords and ladies of Byzantium
> Of what is past, or passing, or to come.

For a number of reasons, my reading of Ann's two books led me to remember that stanza. One reason is that, like Yeats as an older poet, Ann demonstrates in these books the assurance and mastery of poetic technique that time (which permits the maturity of both vision and skill) can bring to talent. Another is the mutual emphasis on song. And—a third reason—Yeats's golden bird is singing of past, present, and future—the underlying melody of both *Orioling* and *The Book of Ga*.

But even as I was thinking of those similarities, I was aware of the immense difference that separates "Sailing to Byzantium" from any poem in Ann's two books. That difference provides me a way to describe *her* song, her voice —that is to say, the interpretation she gives to our human existence. In "Sailing" and other work of his poetic maturity, Yeats conceives of an ideal completion denied us in our brief and fragmented span of living and strives to achieve it through imagination: his bird, gorgeous artifact that it is, sings of the passage of time from a remove, for the bird itself is immortal—beyond nature, beyond change. For Ann, change forms the very fabric of our living and binds us to the changes of the weather, the changes of the seasons. We exist within, and are part of, the flux of nature itself. Her poems make many references to water: the word "flowing" often occurs, "river" even more frequently. In its ceaseless flow, time is conventionally referred to as a river; in Ann's poetry, we have our moment of time within the flow of nature.

The poems of *Orioling* are arranged not in chronological order of their composition but as a demonstration of the ongoing movement in us and all the phenomena of nature. How does one account for that mysterious impulse in humans to create, to sing, during the brief years

that are granted us? The opening poem of *Orioling* provides the title for the collection. The orioles and thrushes
that sing in that poem are not hammered from gold: they
are real birds, and their song is not for our aesthetic pleasure but to claim territory and gain mates. The poem tells
us that human song has a less obvious motivation, for
(among other causes) it issues from the complexity of a
mind aware of itself—from a consciousness always seeking to know how or why it came to be:

> Human, you can't help trying to understand
>   what stalk you flower from, what undertow
> rises in the flutist to quicken with breath
>   the arcs and dips of prior minds, or mind
> itself, playing with fugue, with $E=MC^2$,
>   inventing wheel, organ, flute, B Minor Mass—
> Buddha—the bomb. The song you bear buds
>   under your mind's tongue like a first word.

Though it depends upon mind, human creativity is
analogous to nature's creativity, as the references to "stalk,"
"flower," and "bud" imply. And clearly the repeated use of
nouns and verbs beginning with "b" give these concluding lines of the poem the sound of one explosion after
another: those bursts of energy mark the act of creativity
itself, both in nature and in the human mind. Nature de-
stroys to create anew. The human mind is as capable of
destroying—the nuclear bomb is the prime example—as
it is of inventing useful objects and contemplating, or giving voice to, an encompassing spiritual insight. As for the
"undertow" that "rises in the flutist" as she plays—does it
originate in the unconscious mind, as a kind of genetic or

biological memory of the human genesis in some un-known sea, a memory that, from this moment onward, participates in nature's flow? "Undertow" is a significant word, for it connects the flutist's mind to "prior minds," a phrase that no doubt includes the composer of the piece and previous performers of it and possibly others even farther back in time.

Later poems in the collection amplify what is implied in this opening song. For Ann, it soon becomes apparent, we sing not because we or our artifacts are immortal, but because, as mortal creatures, we respond to the immortal-ity of nature as it flows through us, binding past and future to the ephemeral present. In Ann's own song, such insight has an intimate relationship with all that she values—love (particularly for husband, children, and kinfolk), affection-ate relationships with many others, music, an appreciation of the natural environment, the pleasures of the body. (Her "Tryst for the Adams and Eves" is as sensual a poem as I have read in a long time.) The affirmation—the praise of life—in her poetry is anything but sentimental. Her poems acknowledge not only the bombs we make, but the prejudices we are capable of, and they take into ac-count the barbarous acts that took place in Serbia and Af-ghanistan during the composition of *Orioling*. And they speak, as they must, of human endings. According to a very loose translation of the Roman poet Lucretius's *On the Nature of Things,* "Life lives on / it is the lives, the lives, the lives that die." That is in harmony with Ann's voice; and so is this phrase from a poem by another long-time Ithaca resident, Archie Ammons: "[T]his *is* forever, we are now in it . . ."

Though I have devoted the majority of this review to the song I hear throughout *Orioling,* nearly everything I have said about that collection applies equally to *The Book of Ga.* As a narrative—ostensibly, the story of the life of Ann's grandmother Miriam Nye Loomis, "Ga" being the name given her by her young grandchildren—the book is immediately accessible to any reader. It has the appeal of a film by Ken Burns, for its story is carried by a number of voices that are speaking against a documentary background of photographs, letters, newspaper clippings, and a quarantine notice. From such evidence, Ann constructs her narrative. In it, Miriam grows up in a river town—Marietta, Ohio, at the confluence of the Ohio and Muskingum Rivers. She marries Charley, a photographer from Parkersburg, a nearby city on the other side of the river. They become a family with two children, both boys. Five years after the marriage, Charley dies, a victim of typhoid fever. With her boys, Miriam returns to her childhood home to live with her father, now a widower. A flood inundates much of Marietta. The father remarries; Miriam must be subservient to father and stepmother alike. She escapes to Boston with her children. Here she attends cooking school, to gain the credentials for a job— she gets one at a school for girls—that will support her and the boys. Miriam and the woman who teaches French at the school buy a summer home far from urban confinement. In that Maine farmhouse, close to rivers and lakes and surrounded by fields and woods, her life is happier than it has been since the death of Charley. Now grown, her children depart; then the French teacher marries, leaving her alone. Ultimately, Miriam enters a nursing home: her mind is failing. The moment of her death is not recorded.

It is a simple story, one similar to the lives of many others. And yet it held my attention from beginning to end through the atmosphere it evokes and the poet's ability to convey sensations and emotions. As natural fact and as metaphor, the river runs through this story and is given (much like the chorus in a Greek tragedy) its own voice, its own commentary. As Ann admits in the dedication honoring her grandmother, the story is primarily an imagined one: the intimate details, the feelings ascribed to Miriam, come from the poet's own life. It is true enough that anybody's life—what she or he is doing, feeling, or thinking during a day or a lifetime—is unknowable to another; we gain empathy and understanding of other people through the projection upon them of what we believe and feel ourselves. Miriam's story gains its authenticity through its creator's knowledge that the eternal river that runs through nature runs also, if much too briefly, through each one of us.

The Book of Ga begins with a poem that serves as overture to the narrative. It is titled "What Do You Mean, Praise?" I read that opening poem on the same morning that I heard of Ann's death. Its introductory stanza struck me as if she'd had a premonition of her death, for it begins this way:

> Yes, we could die tomorrow,
> A two-car crash, a second's misjudging of speed.
> Another plane might ram our woods. Anthrax
> could do it, a heart attack, cancer, even a stupid
> fall down the back stairs.

But the second and concluding stanza is the answer given to the hard fact of death, an answer implicit in both volumes under review:

> Haven't we always been in line
> for some kind of ending? It's enough for now
> that our son's on the phone, telling us today's
> griefs, yesterday's joys. What matters is to tug
> lightly on the thin line of his voice, stretch it
> over the hills and woods—what pulls between us
> will not break. This must be what praise is, singing
> the young men our bodies began, who go on
> in this world with their wives, girls, boys,
> the mothers and fathers who go on in us, too,
> and ancestors we never knew who dwell unsuspected
> in our corpuscles and ganglions, smiling us,
> weeping us, walking with us all our lives long.

Not everything carried along in our blood and nerves from the past is benign, of course. A single word in the opening stanza—"anthrax"—reminds us of the plagues we are capable of visiting upon each other. The affirmation at the ending encompasses that, though. Is this poem sufficient consolation, for those who knew and admired Ann? For her, it was; for us, it will have to do.

11 Rereading Ammons's Long Poems

Nearly all the book-length poems of A. R. Ammons were written on adding-machine tape that unrolled during their composition on his old typewriter. To compose a poem on a continuous strip of paper is to write it either without revision or with the revision a part of its ongoing movement. Ammons's long poems are journals of a particular sort, the record of a consciousness focused on the transcription into words of the associations it is currently making—a consciousness capable of contradictions, moments of brilliant illumination as well as moments of comic absurdity, self-deflation, and depression.

Ammons—Archie to his acquaintances—was a prolific poet. He wrote book after book of poems of various lengths, one collection consisting of poems so brief that some are epigrams or puns *(The Really Short Poems of A. R. Ammons).* "Coward," for example, contains five words: "Bravery runs in my family". Another, called "Their Sex Life," requires an additional word: "One failure on / Top of another". These two poems reflect the pure fun Archie could find in words and phrases, while others, like

"Small Song," carry that playfulness a step further into an impression with the haunting quality of a fine haiku: "The reeds give / way to the / wind and give / the wind away".

That quality, along with much else, exists in the collections of poems of a more conventional length. Though not in a collection, one such poem—the dedicatory poem to Harold Bloom that precedes the book-length *Sphere*—strikes me as one of the grandest poems written in English in the twentieth century, moving as it does through narrative to an end made inevitable by its action. Though they vary in intensity, I admire Archie's achievements in the shorter forms so much that they influenced my response to his book-length poems. In reading the long poems as they became available over the years, I found myself always looking for the more concentrated poems they contained, individual poems often so lyrical that I thought of them as arias in an opera that went on too long. The remainder of the material struck me as a series of recitatives—that is to say, mere prose pieces, however carried along these segments might be in the rhythm that marks the whole work. To me, the book-length poems resembled the notebooks poets sometimes keep which give us an insight into what goes on in their minds as they are searching for the ideas and images that, once discovered, will burst into creative song. I wanted to hear those songs, without being privy to the process that created them.

Probably the prejudice I brought to my reading of these long poems is shared by others who think of the ideal poem as a concentrated expression that manages—

through the author's selection and ordering of its images, through those sounds that become soundings—to imply so much more than its apparent subject permits that it expands in the reader's mind, becoming, paradoxically or not, an expression of what is beyond the ability of language to convey.

My response to the long poems was complicated by my attitude to my own writing. I am a writer of prose rather than poetry, a prose writer who is particularly dependent upon the spiritual resources of personal memory to justify and connect the various autobiographical experiences I am recalling. At the very least, I want my words and phrases to pay tribute to a unity or wholeness that lies beyond my ordinary life, and to do that to the best of my ability I revise as I go along. Archie was my friend and colleague over the decades, and I felt, in my private conversations with him as well as in his poetry, the kind of mutual, if unstated, understanding that one has for another whose intuitions or feelings are similar, however different the circumstances of their lives or their political leanings. He was a poet and I wrote prose, so I never felt myself in competition with him, never experienced envy at his growing fame—though I admit I was puzzled that it had much to do with the book-length poems that he turned to with greater frequency in his later years. And I also confess that my initial intent in writing this essay was to rescue the arias from the recitatives that surrounded them.

To achieve such a goal, though, meant that I had to reread those book-length poems, to give them a more attentive reading than I had managed during Archie's lifetime. They contain some typos that he missed and some repetitions that he might not have intended—though given this mode of writing, it is hard to determine that. (He once told me, with apparent surprise at the fact, that the book editors he worked with never suggested changes of any kind.) The width of the tape determines the length of a line in such books as *Tape for the Turn of the Year* (1965), *Garbage* (1993), and *Glare* (1997). In *Sphere* (1974), the lines are somewhat longer, for here Archie seems to have used conventional typewriter paper, his line endings determined by the bell that rang in accordance with the right margin he had set. In these long poems, Archie sometimes complains of the restraint he has imposed upon himself by this method, but in interviews published in local papers he remarks that they provide the discipline poets once found in more conventional forms, such as the sonnet. In rereading the later book-length poems, I could see that he had developed an intuitive control of his self-imposed form that had been lacking in *Tape*, his fledgling attempt—the one responsible for my prejudgment of the others. In the later poems, the line lengths vary from one book to the next, for the tapes are of differing widths. Combined with stanza lengths that also vary from book to book, the lines capture a mental rhythm in keeping with the thoughts and feelings being expressed.

Technical matters of this sort constitute what I first noticed in rereading the long poems. Necessary though they may be to the greater appreciation I now have for those poems, such matters, discussed with pertinent examples from the poems, wouldn't make for lively reading in a personal essay like this one. Instead, I will engage in the kind of associative digression that Archie himself continually employs. The question of what constitutes a proper line seems to be of extraordinary importance to poets, particularly those who have dispensed with traditional forms. I once invited Denise Levertov to Cornell as a participant in a yearlong festival devoted to Chekhov. A quarrel over this issue of the line had brought a disruption of the friendship between Archie and Denise, something they both regretted. Archie readily agreed to have dinner with Denise and me at the Statler Hotel on the Cornell campus and accompanied me to the nearby house where she was staying. They were happy to see each other. My attempt at peacemaking would have been successful had not Archie stopped to admire a bed of yellow flowers as we were walking to the hotel. "My, aren't those lovely flowers, Denise?" he said. "What do you suppose they are?" She replied, "I thought you were a nature poet, Archie. Those are *daffodils.*" The frigidity following that exchange withered the bloom of their rediscovered pleasure in each other's company. At dinner, they wouldn't speak to each other, addressing all their comments to me.

Unlike the book-length poems that follow, *Tape* concludes with a summary of the journey the reader has taken with him, the final entry containing these lines:

> . . . I
> showed that I'm sometimes
> blank & abstract,
> sometimes blessed with
> song: sometimes
> silly, vapid, serious,
> angry, despairing:
> ideally, I'd

> be like a short poem:
> that's a fine way
> to be: a poem at a
> time: but all day
> life itself is bending,
> weaving, changing,
> adapting, failing,
> succeeding:

In rereading those lines, I saw them as Archie's reply from the grave to my objection that he was providing the process along with the songs that emerged from it. So it is life itself, life in all of its changes—that is, life as a *process* —that is his subject, and it is a falsification of whatever constitutes "truth" or "reality" to freeze into ideal form any segment of it. He expresses such a view elsewhere, as in these lines from *Sphere:*

> . . . I don't know about you,
> but I'm sick of good poems, all those little rondures
> splendidly brought off, painted gourds on a shelf: give me
> the dumb, debilitated, nasty, and massive, if that's the
> alternative: touch the universe anywhere you touch it
> everywhere . . .

—though here, of course, he is moving beyond his or anybody's life to an expression that may sound metaphysical but has a basis in scientific knowledge of the elements from which we, and everything that surrounds us, are composed. But to "touch the universe anywhere" is not to immobilize it, for everything in nature (upward from the electrons of the atom and downward to the strange behavior of the smallest particles) is in motion.

Archie studied biology at Wake Forest University, and for the rest of his life was alert to ongoing scientific investigation, to its continuing discoveries and puzzlements— responding especially to those, I would guess, that are connected to his poetic sensibility and knowledge of himself as a person of changeable moods who meanwhile is moving through life to the death that is foreshadowed by the various ailments of his later years. I'm revealing no secrets in saying that Archie's ego was strong and yet tender to slights (like the one he perceived as he was trying to renew his friendship with Denise), or that he felt anger and some long-held resentments as well as generosity, love, and compassion: his own poetry testifies to that and recognizes (especially toward the end of his career) his failings.

It would be reductive, though, to say that Archie's altering emotional states explain his mode of composition in the long poems or in any of the others. All of us demonstrate mutability as we move toward death, though we assume (I know I do) that a constancy of belief or character holds, despite all changes. In opening a needed and especially rewarding essay about Archie's "heart," about the depth of his feelings for others, Roger Gilbert says that readers of Archie's poetry realize "that he has a formidable brain. . . . No other contemporary poet has presented himself so unabashedly as a *thinker* as well as an artist." It is true—something Archie is as aware of as is any reader— that he was drawn to abstractions to a far greater degree than most of us. In rereading the book-length poems, the ones that permit the development or orchestration of those abstractions, it struck me more forcefully than in the past that motion—not linear motion, but motion in the shape of arcs and curves—is essential to everything else the abstractions (as well as the poems themselves) contain. The curves have a basis in knowledge that the universe is expanding, that space itself curves—possibly back on itself. Even "salience," a favorite word in the poems, has its physical equivalent, for example in the jutting forth of energy from the radiant but self-consuming globular mass that permits us life; in its human equivalent, such projections represent the extent to which we can rise on occasion above the ceaseless motion of our lives and of everything of which we are part to gain a clarity of perception or at least to perceive the curve of the horizon that still may limit our seeing.

Many of us who knew Archie have commented on the similarity between his poetry and the nature of his conversation, particularly in his daily coffee-house discussions with friends. His conversation digressed from any current topic, leading to remarks as unexpected as they were either serious or comic (and frequently bawdy: sex for Archie could be as ridiculous as it was crucial to human continuation and human song). The abstractions found in his long poems, though, are not part of the conversational play that he enjoyed and, I think, needed, for the sake of human contact and the insight of others. (In the poem "Summer Place," he says, ". . . I don't want to be by myself: I don't / want anybody else to be by himself much: I don't mind being / alone: it's loneliness that gets me . . .") Those intellectual abstractions, part of the solitary poet's thoughts as he sat at his typewriter (and removed as they are from more purely human considerations), are crucial, I would guess, to one of the reasons he gives for writing the long poems—that (as he says in *Glare*) the act of concentration, even more than the thinking itself, ". . . means / the attention is directed outside / and focused away from the self, away / from obsessive self-monitorings" and all the "misery" waiting to be recalled. That Archie's memory could bring him torment is apparent in his perverse invocation, earlier in this same poem, to the "great mother of the muses" (Mnemosyne) to help him forget a memory from childhood he won't clarify, though it probably refers to the burial of a younger brother; to help him forget the memory of a feeling that however

> fleeting is carved in stone across
> the gut: I can't float or heave it
>
> out: it has become a foundation:
> whatever is now passes like early
>
> snow on a warm boulder: but the
> boulder over and over is revealed,
>
> its gritty size and weight a glare:
> rememberers of loveliness, ruddy
>
> glees, how you cling to memory, while
> haunted others sweat and wring out
>
> the nights and haste about stricken
> through the days . . .

My quotation here is as lengthy as it is to communicate its power, as part of one of the many poems I had initially chosen as examples of the arias that are self-sufficient (or nearly so). In writing this particular song, did Archie have in mind such extollers of memory as I, who find in memory

—however painful certain of the events that are recalled—the desire for unity and oneness that defines the soul?

This essay, like Archie's long poems, is a contemplative process, and what I didn't realize until this moment—not at a typewriter, but at the computer that aids my revisions—is that the major abstractions in Archie's work, whatever their scientific basis, serve him in the same spiritual capacity that memory serves me. That is to say, they serve a purely human need—the need of the psyche for union, for a oneness beyond our mortal grasp. If everything in nature is in motion, the forms of that motion to be represented in arcs, curves, and saliences; if the universe has been expanding since its creation from an apparent nothingness, where is the center to be found? At any given moment, right here, or anywhere. (After all, to "touch the universe anywhere," is to "touch it everywhere.")

And what is true of space is equally true of time. *Garbage* contains a meditation on a number of interrelated matters, the question of meaning and meaninglessness being the central strand. It includes these lines:

> . . . it is
> fashionable now to mean nothing, not to exist,
> because meaning doesn't hold, and we do not exist
> forever; this *is* forever, we are now in it . . .

That's a brave statement from one who, as he grew older, frequently thought of the finality of death. And it is especially brave, given the context in which it is found, for he has just been referring to space as well as time—to the immensity of the cosmos, to "the terror of the / unimaginably empty and endless," to "the core-fire of the galaxy" which permits us—"cellular brushfires" that we are—to "burn cool in a way-off arm."

Whatever burns consumes its fuel: in the universe, as in any closed system, entropy increases as available energy decreases. Stars shrink and die, humans die and their bodies shrink: for both, silence ensues from the loss of motion and light. Of course, even though the universe itself eventually may return to its beginnings in the silent emptiness, new stars and new humans are constantly being born from dust, cosmic or otherwise. Though this phraseology is mine, knowledge of a similar sort is included in Archie's abstractions about motion and has its psychical equivalent in his views about poetry and his own poetics. "The purpose of the motion of the poem," he says in *Sphere,* is to bring the "focused, awakened mind" to "no-motion" where that mind can "touch the knowledge that / motions are instances of order and direction occurring / briefly in the silence that surrounds . . ." The lines that follow stress the importance of silence to renewed creativity, and the passage concludes with an apostrophe addressed "to the spirit-being, great one in the world / beyond sense . . ."

Many writers that I admire—from Augustine to Annie Dillard—have been attracted to silence, as if in silence one can hear the voice of God. Archie's abstractions might be his way of recasting the religious beliefs so prevalent in the rural and impoverished North Carolina of his childhood. To my knowledge, no other poet has constantly struggled against the insignificance that science has brought to us by using science itself to provide us with a sense of a possible unity pervading the cosmos.

Archie's abstractions might seem a cold comfort, at best; but I find them linked to the warmth of the "heart" that Roger Gilbert so properly emphasizes. *Glare,* his final long poem, opens with a return to his long-standing preoccupation with the vastness of the cosmos, one of whose errant motions—in the shape of a boulder, say—might bring an end to all our activities long before Earth is consumed by the sun whose expanding size will foreshadow its own diminution in death. Given such an ultimate cessation, though, "it is not careless to become too local." In the broadest sense, this means that if ". . . the greatest god / is the stillness all the motions add / up to, then we must ineluctably be / included . . .", and ". . . it is / nice to be included, especially from / so minor a pew . . ." In a more specific sense, such insight gives significance to all our endeavors to learn and know everything about the landscape now lying before us; and at least for me, it gives significance to the humble details from Archie's life that follow this abstraction, details with intimate connections to the lives of others: ". . . peanut butter and soda crackers / and the right shoe soles . . ." for icy sidewalks. It is so obvious that I shouldn't need to add that meditations of this sort, no matter how abstract, are connected to Archie's compassion and love, as well as to his need for informal conversations with friends.

Archie's beliefs are to be found in his abstractions; whatever the modifications that may come to them, their details are consistent from the first long poem to the last. His voice remains an affirmative one, though the struggle for affirmation becomes more pronounced after *Sphere,* the most affirmative of them all. *Glare* contains two sections, the first of which, "Strip," shows Archie at the height of his powers, as my references to it indicate; the following and much briefer section demonstrates, above all else, his need—his stubborn will—to go on, despite his declining health and the drugs that seem to be inhibiting his ability to remember, to make quick associations. Nevertheless, its title, "Scat Scan," is a triple pun, the most obvious being its connection to a CAT scan, one of which probably helped in the diagnosis of his own ailments; but "scat" is also a jazz term for singing in which meaningless syllables are improvised, the voice joining the other instruments. Improvisation has always been part of Archie's explorative process. (Its importance to him, in writing as in life, is emphasized here in his comment to himself, ". . . if you can't get going you / might as well get gone, goodbuddy . . .") The third pun, of course, is in the reference, however ironical, to the excrement of wild animals.

But this section, whatever the faults or hesitancies caused by poor health, concludes with a song as lyrical as any of his devising, one which considers the structures we need for our upholding, and asserts they are made

                                  . . . of no
    earthly thing but of will, blank will, which

    acquires nor wields weight but simply insists
    that it is as it is, right through the ruins of

    truth which melts to reservation and contradiction
    right through the rigors of all loss, no more

    nothing than the nothing at the end it joins: . . . .

This song is part of all of Archie's singing:

> . . . it is a sad song but
> it sings and wants to sing on and on and when
>
> it can no more it wants someone else to sing:
> to sing is everything but it is also specifically
>
> to dive the stave into marshy passageways and
> bring relief and the future singers in

A celebration of Archie's achievements—an "Ammons-fest"—was held for him at Cornell in April 1998. It was the kind of large public event that, despite his appreciation of sensitive and informed praise, he always dreaded. (His health was continuing to decline, and Adam Law, his physician as well as mine, was in attendance, for he admired Archie's poetry and the mind that it revealed while worrying ever more about his condition.) Archie had donated his papers to the Cornell archives, and to express its gratitude, the library held a reception for him. That reception required a brief response from him, and he probably gave a gracious one; but all I can remember from it is that he said I was responsible for bringing him to Cornell. When I objected that this wasn't wholly true, he said that yes, it was: the matter was settled, at least in his mind.

After the celebration was over, I wondered at the reason why Archie had said what he did. Could he have realized, from my words with him at the time he gave his initial reading at Cornell—a reading that so impressed many of us that we wanted this then shy and obscure poet to join the faculty—that I felt a particular kinship with him?

I hope so; it certainly accounts for the nature of this essay, and of all that I learned while writing it.

III

An Essay on Politics

The improbable title of a novel of mine published in 1987—*Kayo: The Authentic and Annotated Autobiographical Novel from Outer Space*—may give a sense of the spirit in which it was written. It was such a departure from anything I'd previously published that reviewers who had liked my earlier work didn't know what to make of it. A novel transmitted from a distant planet that is a mirror image of our own, it is a reflection of the absurdity and entrapments of politics, as practiced by presidents and professors alike—by all those in power who find themselves caught up in the sticky webs of their own logic. One critic attacked it as self-indulgent. I suppose it is, if by that one means that the writer enjoyed every moment of its composition, finding much fun in whatever came to his mind from one paragraph or chapter to the next. Because its bumbling hero models himself on his planet's Don Quixote, his idealistic misadventures are too benign for bitter political satire. Still, I felt an almost exalted relief in giving expression at last to the major irritant behind *Court of Memory* as well as other books I'd written during the Cold War decades.

Following the publication of *Kayo,* political matters have often kept me sleepless, but I've found that any attempt to put politics in bed with a personal essay so compromises the gentler partner that the coupling is akin to rape. Except for several essays, one of which follows, politics has not been the subject of my shorter work.

12 Some Views about Cuba for the Delegation That Couldn't Visit

Recently, I was in the back seat of a Russian military vehicle—a kind of jeep. A gentle rain had commenced, and the jeep was stuck behind other military vehicles in the clay of a remote Cuban hillside in the mountainous province of Guantanamo. In addition to my wife, the other passengers in that jeep were an eighty-two-year-old former Unitarian minister and his younger travelling companion. Three of us were the oldest members of the group from the United States and Canada who had just been guests at a plentiful banquet prepared by Taino Indians. Our group of forty-odd people included Jean's and my son, Cris, as well as five high-school students from Kansas City accompanied by their teacher; but the majority of the contingent were Indians themselves—most of them from reservations in the United States and Canada, though a few (descendents of Caribbean Tainos) lived in major American cities.

Indians—whether they are, say, Navajos from the American West or Tainos from Cuba—treat elders with a respect that is quite unlike the treatment accorded to senior citizens in most parts of the United States, where it chiefly amounts to a discount on theater tickets and hotel rooms. And the special attention given to elders seems a part of Cuban culture itself. Certainly, the four of us in that jeep were accorded a special privilege. A general in the Cuban army—one whose exploits in his teens had made him a hero of the Cuban Revolution and who had provided our group with the four-wheel-drive vehicles required for this visit over deeply rutted and seemingly impassable roads to the Taino settlement of Communidad de la Rancheria—motioned our driver out of his seat, took his place, and then expertly maneuvered our vehicle around the others slipping sideways in the clay, gunned the engine and sent us careering up the hill, around and through mudholes and over rocks to the road above. That general—Francisco Gonzales Lopez, known to Cubans as Pancho—is maybe sixty-five himself, but slender as a young athlete. He gave us a smile and then left us sheltered against the drizzle under the canvas canopy of the jeep to see if the drivers of the other vehicles had learned anything from his example. Though they (including the driver of the big truck that carried the majority of our party) had instructed their passengers to walk up the hill on a separate path, they indeed had learned, for all the other vehicles soon roared up, even though the wet clay was as slick as ice.

Our tour group was the fifth in a series of cultural encounters under the rubric of "Indigenous Legacies of the Caribbean" that José Barreiro has led in Cuba. Barreiro is the editor of the fine journal *Native Americas* and a personal friend; I serve as an advisory editor of his magazine —a mostly honorary post. A native of Cuba, of Taino descent himself, Barreiro and others for years have patiently been laboring to resurrect the Tainos from the extinction to which Cuban and other historians, anthropologists, and ethnobiographers formerly consigned them. Like the previous trips guided by Barreiro, this one was sponsored by Indigenous World Tours, based at the Indian reserve near Toronto called Six Nations of the Grand River. The particular subject for the 2001 group was presented to us as "music, plants, and healing," much of it, but not all, related to Taino practice and knowledge.

The Tainos in Cuba and elsewhere in the Greater Antilles, having never lost their culture or their sense of their spiritual connection with the natural world despite their decimation and enslavement by Spanish colonizers, were now regaining their lost language and reclaiming the identity that had long been denied them. Our visit to the Tainos living at La Rancheria, made possible through the military vehicles of the Cuban government, was the most recent acknowledgment of their identity. The indigenous peoples from Canada and the United States in our party obviously saw in the Tainos a mirror of their own past treatment by those who had, through weapons and sheer numbers, conquered them, and saw in them too their own cultural perseverance. Some of the Native Americans in our party were so moved by the warmth and generosity of their counterparts living in that small collection of buildings that their eyes became moist. For that matter, the rest of us were also affected. The remoteness of the thatch-roofed dwellings, the lovely vistas of the surrounding mountains, and the fecundity of the gardens impart to the settlement an idyllic quality that resonates in the various Edenic myths (and possibly the biological memories) shared by otherwise diverse humans.

The Spaniards found the Tainos a peaceful and inno-cent people, generous in their offerings to strangers— qualities that those we met at La Rancheria still possess. (Columbus noted that such characteristics would make the natives good servants and slaves.)

Our contingent was part of a charter flight that flew nonstop from Toronto to Santiago de Cuba, the island's second-largest city. Though it was our son's fourth trip to Cuba, Jean and I were seeing it for the first time. Still, for Cris as well as us, this trip was unusually rewarding. For me, the trip was an enlightening experience, with so many events and scenes to absorb that I recaptured in my eightieth year the feeling I had as a child that time barely moves—that even a single lovely summer afternoon has an eternality about it. Here we were on a large island only ninety miles from Key West, another island (though a tiny and flat one) familiar to my wife and me from our fre-quent winter visits there. But Cuba remains an alien land, one whose political system apparently is considered so suspect, despite the downfall of Communism in the for-mer Soviet Union, that the United States still makes it dif-ficult for its citizens to travel there. (Wanting to go from Cuba to Key West by a more direct route, my wife and I found it cheaper and less of a hassle to fly back to Toronto and, after returning home, take a second flight.)

Shortly before we left for Cuba, I read a brief newspaper account about a delegation from the U.S. Congress that had been denied permission by our State Department to visit that nation. Our own experiences provided us with some perspectives—not only on the Tainos, but on the Socialist experiment in Cuba generally—that I wish had been made available to our elected representatives. I say this even though I know that one can get only a partial insight from a week spent in the eastern provinces of Santiago and Guantanamo—the Oriente region that is the present and ancestral home of the Cuban Tainos. (The isolation of Guantanamo's forested mountains provided refuge for revolutionaries—including the Cuban national hero José Marti, who fought to free the island from Spanish control in the late nineteenth century, and Fidel Castro and his growing band of supporters, who in 1959 successfully overthrew Fulgencio Batista, a dictator that the United States accepted and at least tacitly supported for his defense of American investments in the land and industries.)

By comparison with the United States, Cuba is an exceptionally poor country. But it has no vast assemblage of hillside shacks with their open sewers and manifest poverty that surround so many South American cities, none of the manifest social and economic inequalities of many other countries, democratic in theory as some of them may be. The lack not only of ghettoes but of any apparent discrimination based on skin color makes Cuba a model that the United States should study; it suggests that much of our continuing racial discrimination stems from, or at least is reinforced by, economically based class distinctions. In the cities and villages we visited, the houses might be crowded together, the dwellings small if not tiny, their metal roofs rusted and patched; but these houses have electricity, water, and sanitary facilities, and their interiors are clean and adequately furnished.

During that week, we visited three elementary schools and one clinic. The school buildings were not large, consisting of several classrooms opening upon a courtyard, each room with neatly arranged chairs and desks, maps and pictures on the walls, and modest supplies (our group augmented them with tablets and crayons) for drawing and writing. Such schools are the foundation of an educational system that can lead to graduate studies in the various disciplines—and that has given the people a remarkably high level of literacy. Each school had prepared for our visit, offering us local foods for refreshment and presenting us with short plays and poems the students had memorized. In addition, and in keeping with one of the interests of our group, the children at one school had arranged a display of native herbs. They took turns, one earnest child after another explaining to us the medicinal uses of each plant. Cris kept a detailed journal for each day of our trip, and what he wrote of his impressions coincides with mine: "To look at the faces of the students and their teachers is all it takes to see that this is a very nurturing environment. There is no evidence of cliques, or rebellion to school authority, or fear of any sort. Rather, they seem bathed in the richness of a common Cuban identity of diverse cultural roots."

Like the educational system, health services are offered at no cost to all Cubans. The clinic we visited is part of the scattering of buildings that include a school at Caridad de los Indios; both clinic and school serve the mountainous area that encompasses the Taino settlement we were yet to visit. The young doctor, the three nurses, and the pharmacist, all of them in their white medical uniforms, showed us the examining room, the room for consultations with patients and family members, and the pharmacy. (The shelves of that room were filled far more with herbal mixtures than with antibiotics and other hard-to-obtain manufactured drugs; many of the herbs were grown in the garden near the entrance of the clinic.)

Critically ill patients, the doctor told us, were transported by ambulance out of the mountains to the major hospital in Guantanamo City; the majority were treated, apparently with a high rate of success, at the clinic. Between the scheduled appointments that pregnant women had at the clinic, the doctor or another of the health workers would visit them at home. He told us that more than forty women had given birth in the past year, and that all the mothers and babies had survived. He also said that a recent nutritional study of the inhabitants of the area had found one person who was malnourished and another who was underfed; upon being supplied with a more nutritious diet, the health of both improved. (Later, I learned that Cuban doctors earn the equivalent of twenty-five dollars a month, not enough, particularly in the cities, to support a family. They are not supposed to augment their income from other employment, though some may indeed violate that rule; but in remote Caridad de los Indios, what other employment could a doctor ever find? Like the doctor, the other health workers took pride in their mutual accomplishments, and perhaps that is the intangible but real reward for their dedication.)

In advance of the feast prepared for us later in the day at La Rancheria, the cacique—or chief—of that indigenous community, Panchito Ramirez, led his Taino people in a series of traditional songs, including a particularly haunting one we had heard on earlier occasions that begins, "Oh, Ma-Ma," a celebration of Mother Earth. After the singing, he spoke to us of the seven principles of the Taino cosmic view—earth, sky, sun, moon, stars, water, and wind—as an introduction to the spiritual importance of the tobacco ceremony he then performed. He blew cigar smoke in each of the four directions before sprinkling tobacco on the coals of a fire—a ceremony that had much in common with a blessing that a member of our party (a lawyer and judge and former chief of the Navajo nation) had a day or so earlier performed for our group. (Geographically dispersed as they may be, Indians must share this ritual as homage to, and request of blessing and purification from, the natural world from which they, like all of us, have come. Years ago, I attended a similar ceremony—performed by a Mohawk who at the time headed the American Indian program at Cornell—that preceded the construction of a residence and meeting space for Native Americans and other students.)

Then Panchito—we were accustomed to calling him by that name, for as a friend of Barreiro with an intimate knowledge of medicinal herbs, he had accompanied us elsewhere on our tour, leading us one pleasant afternoon through the tropical foliage of an island in the Toa River near Baracoa where medically useful plants were abundant—offered the cigar to his guests. General Gonzales Lopez was among those to participate in the ritual. (It may have been more than a diplomatic act on his part, one acknowledging his good will; for he, like the Tainos, has an ecological awareness, and is a leader of Cuba's efforts at reforestation.)

Later, in a brief speech intended more for the American visitors than our Taino hosts, he spoke of the reclamation, including reforestation, of land long ravaged by foreign intruders who cut the trees and eroded the soil in their search for profit. Cuba is a small nation, he said, one striving to redress, for the sake of its people, the environmental damage inflicted upon it in the past. Shouldn't its autonomy be respected by larger nations? In attempting to impair Cuba's economy, the American embargo had not kept his country from its efforts to restore the land, but it had certainly impeded the progress. He was willing, he said, to try to answer any questions we might have.

I felt I was speaking for our group when I replied—through Barreiro, acting as interpreter—that it was difficult to ask questions about a talk with which one is in complete agreement. Now that I'm back home, I remain in agreement; I imagine, though, that it required the withdrawal of Soviet agricultural assistance—which included the large tractors, harvesting equipment, and chemicals that are also part of large farming operations in the United States—before ecological improvements could be undertaken to remedy the damage originally inflicted by colonial invasion and later by capitalistic enterprise. To avoid the probability of large-scale hunger, Cuba intensified its use of the practices of its indigenous people—who, long before Columbus arrived, had developed communal farming methods that, without chemicals or artificial fertilizers, produced varied and bountiful crops. The benefits of those traditional methods surrounded us even as we talked, benefits which Cuban agricultural scientists have abetted through biological agents and other natural means in their search for self-sufficiency in food.

Such efforts seem to have succeeded surprisingly well. The daily Cuban diet may be simple, but it is obviously adequate: the Cubans we met or observed on the streets were as well nourished as they were adequately (the women sometimes colorfully) dressed. In Baracoa, the picturesque harbor town at the eastern edge of Cuba, an English-speaking Cuban told me that dogs are indicators of a people's food supply. He said that when food shortages in Cuba were most severe, in the period following the withdrawal of Soviet aid, many people had little food, and the dogs slowly disappeared. "Now, look," he instructed me, pointing to the little white mongrel wagging his tail at our feet and all the other dogs scampering about by themselves.

We spent three days in Baracoa, listening to music at night and attending daily panel discussions on recent discoveries, in America and Europe as well as Cuba, of the therapeutic effects of plants (including the high-bush cranberries by our pond at home, planted long ago in a family project to provide fruit for obstinate birds who continue to spurn the berries) and even of an extract made from scorpion venom, which someday may be used to treat inoperable brain tumors. As was true wherever we travelled, the inhabitants of Baracoa were friendly, greeting us with warm smiles. Maybe the balmy weather had something to do with it, but the people we passed on the streets seemed happier—and certainly more vivacious—than do those on the streets of upstate New York even when they're not blanketed in snow.

Since our return, I have been thinking about the impressions the week's immersion in another culture made upon me—far too many for inclusion here. Its economy is not so precarious as it was, but Cuba remains a struggling nation: a dream of nearby prosperity has sent any number of Cubans fleeing to our shores, and some have died in the attempt. As a writer, I have the freedom to say anything I want, including the criticism implicit in this account of American materialism and the inequalities and injustices that stem from it. (Of course, to criticize America, even if somebody reads an essay like mine plucked from the vast flow of entertainment and information provided by our media, is as harmless an activity as popping a cork against the armored plates of a battleship.) But a criticism of its revolution would be censored in Cuba, which has its own righteous ideas of what is politically correct; writers have been imprisoned for such attacks.

No, I don't want to live in Cuba—but I am intrigued by its accomplishments despite formidable obstacles. Whatever its flaws, the virtues to be found on that nearby island could enlighten us in our quest to better our powerful, still-fortunate nation.

IV

A Story for a Child

Like most adults, I wish, now and then, to escape to a more innocent time or condition, one without daily responsibilities or anxieties about the human world, my own country, and the people I love. On rare occasions, we are granted that wish. The story that follows, written more than thirty-five years ago for my youngest child, celebrates such an occasion. Last year, I came across that old manuscript. As a kind of postscript, I added to it a summary covering the passage of years, and sent copies to all those middle-aged adults who are portrayed in it as school-age children or college undergraduates.

Innocence provides us no lasting shelter, but it seems appropriate to me to end this collection with an account of a moment in time in which innocence prevails, much as it does in "Idyll," an essay in the opening section.

13   The Island of Ice

(November 1967)

At the farmhouse ten miles from Ithaca, the morning began the way all November mornings began. Jean, the mother, woke up at 6:44, a minute before the alarm was set to ring, turned off the alarm switch, and slept again.

The house was very still.

At seven o'clock, Jean woke up, jumped out of bed, staggered to the closet for her housecoat, and went calling from door to door: "Jimmy, it's seven," "Cris, it's seven," "Kay, it's seven," "Larry, it's seven."

The father, Jim, listened as she called the family, closed his eyes and went back to sleep, as was his custom. He *said* he stayed in bed so that everybody who was in a hurry to get up and away could use the bathrooms without having to wait for him. And so he could fall back into slumber as if he were doing a good deed. Of course, if he had been a farmer instead of a college teacher he would have already been at work, milking cows or feeding the livestock.

Jean pattered downstairs to turn up the thermostat and to fill and plug in the coffeepot. She took a shower, got dressed, and went from door to door, knocking on each one and saying more urgently: "Jimmy, it's seven-twenty," "Cris, it's seven-twenty," "Kay, it's seven-twenty," "Larry, it's seven-twenty." And, standing in the middle of the hallway, she cupped her hands to her lips and cried: "John Crispin and James Clayton: hurry *up* or you'll miss the bus." She and Jim used the full names of their children whenever they wished to stress the importance of what they were saying to them.

And then she went back downstairs to the kitchen, to set the table, which included putting vitamin pills by Jimmy's plate and Cris's plate and, at the corner of the table, two little piles of change for their lunch money. Then she began making French toast.

At seven-thirty, she stood at the foot of the stairway, cupped her hands again and yelled as loudly as she could: *"Get up."*

Jimmy and Cris tumbled out of their beds, raced toward the bathroom, and collided in front of the door. There followed a debate as to Who Had Got There First. Finally Cris tramped downstairs to the bathroom there, while Jimmy went into the upstairs bathroom. Cris was fifteen and Jimmy seven, and if Jimmy had his way the reason was that Cris, being older, saw the advantage in being gracious.

For the same water pipes served both bathrooms. When Cris turned on the hot water faucet in the downstairs bathroom, Jimmy, taking a quick shower upstairs, discovered his warm water had turned very cold. He appeared, dripping, at the head of the stairs and shouted, "Cris, *turn off your water.*"

It was a morning like any other.

Jean walked out on the porch to look at the thermometer—it was 31 degrees—and to check the wind—damp, with occasional gusts—so she would know whether to take sweaters or winter coats from the closet. She chose the sweaters, and put them on separate chairs near the door. Then she called: "Ten to eight! Ten to eight!"

The bus always came at nine minutes after eight.

Jimmy and Cris ran back to their rooms. Kay tiptoed into the upstairs bathroom and shut the door gently so as not to disturb her Uncle Jim while Larry tramped into the bathroom downstairs. Kay was a student at one of the colleges in Ithaca. Her mother and Jean were sisters. Kay was from Cincinnati and was living at the farmhouse. Larry—Jean and Jim's oldest son—was a freshman at another college in Ithaca, the one at which both his parents worked. Larry lived in a dormitory on campus but usually came home on weekends. Both Larry and Kay took showers at the same time this morning, but Kay, who was a dependable and good-natured girl as well as a guest in the house for a year, did not scream at Larry that her water was cold.

At eight minutes after eight, Cris and Jimmy, each with a scrubbed face, combed hair, and clean clothes, walked calmly into the kitchen, which was heavy with smoke. Jean, whose hair had fallen over one eye, dumped the burned French toast into the garbage bucket and said in her most restrained manner, "Once again you're too late for breakfast, and once again it doesn't matter because once again I've been so busy shouting at you to come that I've burned it. The bus will be here any moment. Hurry, take your vitamin pills with your orange juice and put your lunch money in your pockets—do it *now*, Jimmy, so your teacher won't have to pay for your lunch out of her own purse again—and get your sweaters on."

Kay shivered in the shower and returned to her room, humming softly. Larry continued to sing to himself in the shower downstairs, a Simon and Garfunkel song. Jean said again, to nobody in particular, "Hurry! Hurry!"

It could have been any gloomy Monday in November.

But the bus didn't come at 8:09.

Jean made golden brown French toast which Cris and Jimmy leisurely ate, wearing their sweaters. Jean stood by the window watching.

At 8:15, Kay came downstairs with a large pile of books—she had been studying late the night before, as usual—and put them on a corner of the buffet and walked into the kitchen. "Well, this is a nice surprise!" she said, to Cris and Jimmy. They all ate French toast together.

Upstairs, Jim yawned and stretched, rose from bed and had a quick shower (the water still being cold), shaved—and came rushing down the stairs. It was almost 8:30. On his way to the kitchen he heard Larry singing his Simon and Garfunkel song in the downstairs shower; and thinking of his own cold shower, he pounded on the bathroom door and shouted, "For heaven's sake, Larry, turn off the water before you pump the well dry."

Hurrying into the kitchen, he stumbled over his untied shoelaces. "I'm late, I have to be at a committee meeting in half an hour," he cried. "Is the coffee ready?" And then he saw Jimmy and Cris, eating breakfast with Kay. "What's the matter?" he cried accusingly to the two of them. "Did you miss the bus again?"

Jean twisted a curl of hair around a finger before turning away from the window. "*Of course* the coffee's ready at 8:30 in the morning," she said. And she said, "The bus hasn't come."

Jim said, "Something must be up." Whenever anything out of the ordinary happened—for example, when the bus didn't come on time—he always expected a catastrophe of some sort. He said, "I'll see what the radio says." He rushed into the living room, stumbling over his shoelaces, and turned on the radio, trying to find the local station. He always turned on the radio in the living room whenever anything out of the ordinary took place. He never could find the Ithaca station. He listened to a summary of world news from a Syracuse station. Carefully he tied his shoelaces and then walked with dignity into the kitchen. "What a mess, what a *dreadful* mess," he said.

"What's a mess, Uncle Jim?" Kay asked dutifully.

Jimmy said, "Is it about the school bus?"

Jim said, "If *I* were president—"

"Oh," said Cris, "you were listening to the world news again."

Jimmy asked, "Was there anything about our bus on the world news?"

"Forget it," Jim said. He poured himself a cup of coffee and then noticed Jean was missing. "Boys," he asked, "where's your mother?"

"Phoning the bus garage," Cris said. "She thought they would know more about what had happened to the bus than Walter Cronkite would."

Larry came into the kitchen, dressed, humming another Simon and Garfunkel song. "What's for breakfast?" he asked. "I've got to hurry, I have a class."

Kay rose from the table. "So do I," she said. "I have an exam in sociology."

Jim said, "I have to be at a committee meeting. I'm going to be late——"

Jean came into the room. "Nobody's going anywhere," she said. "'There's an island of ice south of Trumansburg all the way to Connecticut Hill.' Those are the words of the man in charge of the buses. School's been cancelled."

"Hurray!" cried Jimmy. "Can you drive down and pick up George? We'll play in the barn."

"Nobody can drive *anywhere*," Jean said. "I can't pick up George or anybody." And she said, "I'm supposed to be at work, too. There was a paper I was supposed to finish today, and slides to be made for a seminar presentation." Jean worked in a biochemistry laboratory. Busy as she was, she never made a fuss about it.

"I simply *have* to take my exam," Kay said.

"I have to get to class," Larry said.

"Ice?" Jim said scornfully, looking out the window. "Clearly there's no ice. I've got to get to a committee meeting." And he stomped to the door. "I'll show you there's no ice," he said, and walked briskly down the porch steps. He nearly lost his balance as he slid on one foot and then on the other all the way down the walk to the road. "It's a good thing I tied my shoelaces," he said, coming into the kitchen for his coffee.

Kay left the kitchen to make a telephone call. Then she put on her coat and picked up her pile of books and came to the kitchen door, with a look of extreme determination. "Goodbye," she said. "God willing, I'll see you tonight."

"You can't go," Jim said in alarm. "You don't have ice like this in Cincinnati. You simply don't know what you're saying."

"Oh yes I do," Kay said. Her voice was firm but polite. "I called a friend in Ithaca, and there's no ice *there*. I'll drive very slowly—I promise you, Uncle Jim—until I get past the ice. *My* Fiat can get me anywhere." She was proud of her little secondhand car.

"If it will start," Larry said. Larry owned a very old Rambler station wagon. It always started. Kay and Larry often argued about which of them had the better car.

"If anybody drives to Ithaca, we all should go together," Jim said. "Wait a minute, Kay, until we work out a plan. The question is, what will we do with Jimmy and Cris?"

"Plans take forever," answered Kay, who had experience with those her uncle made. "I've simply got to go now, Uncle Jim. Why, if I didn't go, my professor would have to make up a special examination, just for me." When Kay was being especially Responsible, she was both very sweet and very obstinate. "Goodbye," she said again, and blew a kiss.

Jean, Jim, Jimmy, Cris, and Larry all crowded at the kitchen window, watching as Kay stepped very carefully over the ice to the red barn on the other side of the road. Soon there came a sputter and then a roar as if a half-dozen motorcycles had all started at once, and blue smoke poured out of the open barn door.

"One thing about Kay's car," Larry said. "You can tell a mile away if it's started."

Kay backed her tiny car out of the barn. She gave a triumphant, even a regal, wave of her hand to her audience at the window, and drove down the road at two or three miles an hour. She drove with two wheels on the road, two wheels on the grassy shoulder for the added traction. Her audience watched as the car grew tinier than ever. Finally, it passed over the crest of a small hill half a mile away.

Larry put on his coat and gathered together his books —a smaller pile than Kay's—and some record albums. "I think I ought to follow her into town," he said. "That way, if anything happens to her car, I can help." He opened the door before anybody could argue. "Goodbye, I'll see you next week," he said.

Jean, Jim, Jimmy, and Cris all watched at the window as Larry backed his car out of the barn much more quickly than Kay had done. After he put on his brakes, the car continued backward, sliding across the road and into the front yard. He waved casually to *his* audience, bumped off the lawn, and drove down the road after Kay, two wheels on the road, two wheels on the grassy shoulder. His car grew smaller and smaller, too, though not so small as Kay's. And it too finally vanished over the crest.

Jean groaned, turning from the window. "I forgot to tell Larry to take his laundry," she said. "Now he won't have any clean shirts or socks."

Jim stomped out of the kitchen. He returned, wearing his coat and carrying his briefcase. He picked up the laundry bag, balancing it on his shoulder. "I'll take his clothes into town," he said grimly.

"There's no point in *your* going," Jean replied. "You're already too late for your committee meeting."

"Well," said Jim, "if Larry followed Kay to help her in case something happened to her car, shouldn't I follow *him* so that I could help them both? Imagine, all three of us driving separate cars into town on the iciest day of the year! All of us too late to do whatever it was we were to do in town! And all because we didn't have time enough to make a reasonable plan!"

Cris giggled.

Jean said calmly, "Sit down and relax before you go. You haven't had any breakfast."

Cris lifted the laundry bag from Jim's shoulder, took his briefcase and coat, and led him to the kitchen table. Then he said to Jean, "You haven't had any breakfast either. Both of you sit down, and I'll make French toast for you."

Jean sat down next to Jim. Cris cracked an egg, spilling some of it over the bowl and down the side of the stove. Jean pretended not to notice. Jimmy stayed at the window, watching.

Just as Jean and Jim were finishing the French toast that Cris had made, Jimmy shouted, "They're coming back!"

Jean, Jim, and Cris joined Jimmy at the window. Kay's Fiat and Larry's Rambler had just come over the crest. Slowly the cars grew larger, each going two or three miles an hour, each with two wheels on the road and two wheels on the shoulder. Kay and Larry drove their cars back into the barn. A final roar and a sputter came from the barn, followed by a wisp of smoke. Kay brought her big pile of books into the house, and Larry brought his books and records.

Kay said, "I got to the bottom of the dip and couldn't get up the other side. Larry almost slid into me. We decided we'd better come back."

"Well," said Jim, "I'm glad you did."

"I *tried*," said Kay cheerfully. "I'm glad that I tried, Uncle Jim."

"Now what will we do?" Jimmy asked. "It's a special sort of day."

"It's a work day," said Jim. "We can *work*." And he picked up his briefcase and walked resolutely into his study.

Kay took her books to her bedroom and began reading her assignments for the week after the next, for she was already a week ahead.

Larry took a book and his phonograph albums into the living room. He put a Simon and Garfunkel record on the turntable, twisted the volume knob to high, and then lay on the couch to read. He always said he read best when the phonograph was playing at full volume.

Jean went into the kitchen, to wash the dishes and clean the stove.

Jimmy walked into the television room. He turned up the volume of the television as far as it would go, so that he wouldn't hear the noise of Larry's music.

Cris wandered around the house with his hands in his back pockets.

Jimmy marched into the living room to turn down the volume of the phonograph.

Larry got up from the couch, turned the volume back up, and walked into the television room to turn down the noise of the cartoon that Jimmy was watching.

Jimmy started to chase Larry. They ran from room to room. The two dogs, Black Judy and Janie, who had been sleeping peacefully in a corner of the kitchen, began to bark. They chased Jimmy and Larry. In alarm, the three cats—Marmalade, Humphrey, and Lucy—jumped from their sleeping places on bookcases and chair backs. Humphrey leaped to the desk where Jim was working, and then to Jim's shoulder.

Cris turned off *both* the phonograph and the television. Larry and Jimmy and the dogs began chasing him.

Jim got up from his desk and came into the hallway, Humphrey on his shoulder. Kay stood at the top of the steps, a book in her hand. Jean walked from the kitchen, carrying a dishrag.

"I must say," said Jim in a hurt voice, as if all the chaos had been directed against him alone, "I must say this is a *very* odd day."

Jean said, "I don't think it's going to be a work day, not at all, not one minute of it."

Jimmy, Larry, Cris, and the dogs ran through the hallway, nobody knowing who was chasing whom. Humphrey jumped from Jim's shoulder to the stairway, scampered up, ran past Kay, and hid in a corner of a closet. Then Jimmy, Larry, and Cris came back, quietly.

Cris said, "Jimmy has an idea."

Larry said, "Unlike some of his ideas, this one isn't wacky."

Jimmy said solemnly, "I've never spent a day in the middle of an island of ice before. I want all of us—" and he looked proudly at Larry and Cris, who had already approved his idea, and then at Kay at the top of the stairs and then at Jean and Jim; and all his words came out in a rush —"Iwantallofustogoice-skating."

Jim said sharply, "What? What did you say?"

Jean said, "The pond's not frozen."

"Skating on the road!" Jimmy cried in triumph. "We can go ice-skating on the road!"

"On a day like this," Jean said thoughtfully, "an idea like that sounds as if it could save us all."

"Hurray!" shouted Jimmy, and strutted toward the closet where the ice skates were kept.

"Come on, Kay," said Larry.

"I'll study," Kay said from the top of the stairs and began to retreat toward her bedroom. "It will be nice and quiet in the house, with all of you out of it."

"We've got extra pairs of ice skates," Larry said. "We'll all skate. Come on, Cris, let's get Kay." And they ran up the stairs to drag her down. She protested all the way. "We don't have much ice in Cincinnati," she said, halfway down. "I can't skate," she said, at the foot of the stairs. But she was laughing as they sat her down in the chair and began lacing a pair of ice skates to her feet.

Larry was the first one to skate down the road. "I've never seen such perfect ice!" he cried. He seemed to move without any effort at all; he skated off in the direction he and Kay had gone in the cars, but at a much greater speed. In a few moments, he was over the crest and gone; but then he was back, racing toward the rest of them.

"Isn't this fun?" cried Kay, but somewhat dubiously, holding on to Jim with one hand and to Jean with the other. Jimmy was so pleased with himself that he lost balance and skidded on his stomach down the road. He had just learned to skate the previous year. Larry jumped over him and then whirled in circles until he stopped.

Cris, who had scientific interests, said, "The weight on the skates melts the surface of the ice: that's why we can glide. If the weather is too cold, the ice won't melt fast enough and you can't slide so far because of the friction. *This* must be the optimum temperature for ice-skating. I wonder what the *exact* temperature is," and he skated toward the house to look at the porch thermometer to see for himself, even though Jean told him twice that it was 31 degrees Fahrenheit.

Larry went back with him, to get hockey sticks and pucks out of the closet.

Jean and Jim began to dance together. They danced in unsteady circles until their skates tangled and they fell. Jean gave Jim a kiss on the cheek as they sat in the middle of the road.

Kay was skating by herself. "Look, I can do it!" she cried. Her ankles buckled with every step, but she looked blissful.

Larry and Cris and Jimmy began swinging their hockey sticks at the puck. Black Judy and Janie tried to catch the puck, but their feet splayed out on the ice, and they sailed across the road and into the grass. Jean and Jim began dancing again, but much more slowly this time. Jimmy skated up to them and burrowed between their coats like a rabbit. It was a habit he had, when he was happy.

The three of them skated together. Jean and Jim suddenly stopped, and catapulted Jimmy beyond them. He flew down the road, chortling. He glided all the way to the apple orchard.

Far down the road, in the opposite direction from Ithaca, Cris saw somebody else skating. "I'd like to skate down to see who that is," he said to Jim.

"Why not?" replied Jim.

Cris skated off.

Jim and Kay and Jean and Jimmy held hands, skating in a line. Kay said, "The exam must be almost over. I should feel guilty for missing it, but I only feel guilty for feeling fine."

Then Larry coaxed Kay into playing hockey with him. She picked up a hockey stick, swung at the puck, missed it, and sprawled on the ice. "That takes care of the last of my guilt," she said, rubbing her hip.

Cris came gliding back. "That was an old man skating," he cried. "He's just gone to visit the Newmans. He's seventy-eight, he told me. And he's getting deaf. I had to shout."

"You're still shouting," Jim observed. Cris often shouted when he was excited.

"He said he normally stays off the road because he's so deaf, he has to stay in the house or yard," he said, trying not to shout. "But there's no traffic, and so he's gone skating to see all his old friends. He stops at one house, and then another. He's been to Perry City, he's been to Mecklenburg." He was beginning to raise his voice again. "He's five miles from home. Imagine that!"

"If I can skate when I'm seventy-eight," began Jim, suddenly discovering his rhyme and going on, "I'll feel so great I'll phone a young date."

"But it's your fate to *have* your mate," said Jean. "She's an untamed Kate who'll hit your pate at a dreadful rate."

"Oh, well," said Jim, at a loss for rhymes.

Cris was the first of them to notice that wind was beginning to blow from the south. He skated up the walk and clumped into the house. He returned in a moment with a furled black umbrella. "It's your umbrella," he said to Jim. "Do you mind if I use it?"

"Of course I mind," said Jim, who often said no before he thought. It was a new umbrella, and one of his boys had broken the last one. But he was enjoying the skating.

"Well," he said, skating backwards and not falling, "I mind, but not so much." He skated forward. "You'll probably break some spokes," he said gruffly. Never had ice been so smooth under his skates. "What are a few broken spokes, anyway?" he asked, pleased by his generosity and at the thought of Cris being carried down the road by the wind. He often said yes by asking rhetorical questions of that sort.

"Can I have an umbrella, too?" Jimmy asked in excitement.

"That's the only one we have," Jean said. "I'm sorry. Do you care, Jimmy?"

"Yes, I care," said Jimmy in a quavering voice. "I care a lot." A battle was going on inside him. "But not so terribly much. Not so terribly, so *awfully* much." He bellowed, as fiercely as he could: "Just remember, Cris: all this fun was *my* idea." And then he laughed, pleased with himself once more.

"Goodbye," said Cris, popping open the umbrella. "This trip has been made possible through the kindness of others." He held the umbrella above and in front of him, and started to move. "I wish to acknowledge——" he began, but he was moving rapidly away. "Goodbye," he cried, gliding so fast he was already at the apple orchard.

Jean, Jim, Jimmy, Larry, and Kay stood in a row, watching Cris speed down the road. He grew smaller and smaller; he passed the Newmans' house, where he had met the old man, and sailed on and on until he became a little straight line holding a tiny dot. And then he was gone.

"When he gets to the end of the island of ice, he'll fall," Jimmy said thoughtfully.

"As if he had come to the edge of the world," Jim said.

"I think he'll see it in time," Jean said. "He'll probably tack down a side road, the way a boat does on the water. He can tack all around the island, and sail home."

They stood silently, looking down the empty road. On most days, the sound of a truck laboring up a hill on the highway a mile away could be heard, at least faintly; but on this day there was no sound whatsoever. Overhead, the clouds moved slowly past, in one giant bank after another. The sun suddenly brightened the slopes of the hills in the neighboring county and lit the summit of Connecticut Hill. They could see in all directions for miles. Nothing stirred.

"I've never *heard* such silence," said Jimmy in a whisper.

"And just think what a hullabaloo we were raising earlier!" Jean said. "'Eat your breakfast,' and 'Where's the bus?' I burned the French toast. The phonograph and the television blaring . . . The dogs and the cats, and all of us in a fret."

Jimmy was looking at Jean. Although he knew the answer, he asked, "Why are you smiling so?"

Jean said, "Because I couldn't go to work, because Jim missed his committee meeting, and Kay her exam and Larry his class . . . Because the bus didn't come, and you and Cris couldn't go to school." She tousled his hair. "I shouldn't say such things, should I? Because here we *are,* on our island of ice. Because, Jimmy, *you* decided we ought to go ice-skating, that's why."

And Jimmy, who had never been happier in his life, and never more embarrassed, lost his balance on purpose and tumbled on the ice.

Soon after Cris had completed his sail on skates, the island of ice melted. The next day the bus came precisely at nine minutes after eight. Swallowing their vitamin pills, struggling into their sweaters, forgetting their lunch money, Jimmy and Cris ran out the door. And so day followed day. Every night, as rain or snow fell, Jim read bedtime stories to Jimmy. One night, Jimmy said to him, "Remember the day we skated on the road? I wish that day were made into a story. I wish you would write it down, saying everything just the way it was."

And Jim did that, the very next day. It became one of the stories that Jimmy liked to have read to him. The next summer, Kay drove off in her car for the last time: the little car grew ever smaller, vanishing over the crest of the hill. Years passed, and one by one Larry, Cris, and finally Jimmy moved away from the old farmhouse, driving away in their own cars to make lives for themselves. As each one left, there were fewer to watch as his car, packed with belongings, vanished over the crest of the hill. Larry and Jimmy married and moved into houses of their own, but Cris finally returned to the farmhouse because he needed land for the herd of goats he had just bought. He wanted to earn his living selling goats'-milk cheese. So many years went by that Jean and Jim became even older than the old man Cris had met on the morning he had skated away, down the ice-slicked country road.

One day Jim was looking through a file drawer near his desk for something he had misplaced when he came across a yellowed typewritten manuscript called "The Island of Ice." He was surprised that once Jean and he had the agility to dance on skates in the middle of the road, with never a fear of broken bones; but what he marvelled at, most of all, was how much fun they'd had, on the morning that the island of ice had kept them from their normal duties. Jimmy, more than anybody else, had made it a morning of magic. And Jim realized that long ago each of his children, sometimes all of them together, had brought many other magical moments to Jean and him. Parents are supposed to teach their children about life, but the children have much to teach them about the wonder and enchantment that life can bring. Long ago, Jim thought he had written a story for his seven-year-old son Jimmy. Now, though, that story seemed to have been one he had written for his own eventual rediscovery in his eighty-first year.

But in uncovering this small treasure from his family's past, he decided that maybe it had been written for all children as well as their parents and grandparents, whether or not they ever had gone ice-skating on a country road.

V

Envoy

14   Nurture for the Damn Ego

In 2001, I wrote "Happy Trails to All," an essay included in the opening section of this collection. For various personal reasons, many of them connected to my age—I was approaching my 80th birthday—I thought my essay would be the last piece I would write. In addition, the editors of the magazines and books who had most welcomed my work over the years had either retired or been replaced when their firms were sold to larger ones. (I remember going into the offices of E. P. Dutton—it had just been taken over by a conglomerate—for an appointment with the editor of a forthcoming book of mine. The editor-in-chief, who once had promised to keep my work in print so long as I lived, saw me enter and asked me to come into his room. At first he walked back and forth, too agitated to speak. Finally, he said, "Jim, I came into this work because I love literature, and I think I can tell whether or not a manuscript is worth publishing. But by God I can't tell how many copies it will sell." A few days later, he resigned.)

Personal memory is the thread underlying nearly everything I've written. Memory, of course, is the faculty that permits us to make associations, to find affinities among seemingly disparate materials. Though as a subjective truth it is capable of error, memory provides the basis for whatever understanding we have of the world and of ourselves, and of the values that either consciously or unconsciously we uphold. The pleasure that writing has afforded me—a physical pleasure, first centered in the stomach and then extending throughout the body and mind—has always come from memory's ability to link, more from elusive feelings than logic, a present moment to earlier ones. I have often wondered why my very body responds so pleasurably to revelations of connections to be found within the myriad details of life, as if those linkages, like food and love, were necessary to it. The only answers to that question I am capable of giving are that the human psyche apparently is in search of a unity, or synthesis, beyond its grasp and that the body responds to many of the associations the mind is capable of making as if those connections are a good. Augustine believed that the human mind carries a memory of God and that it makes us feel good to behave in a way commensurate with that memory. Born many centuries after Augustine, I lack the certitude of his faith; nevertheless, he has been— along with later writers I also admire—a congenial presence while I'm writing.

Since I felt that "Happy Trails to All" would mark the end of my writing career, I used it to sum up a life nearing its conclusion. I wrote it primarily for myself, uncertain that it would ever be published, even though—as the title makes clear—I was hoping that others might read it, finding in it some application to their own journeys. I wrote it as a kind of testament to life, not art; for I've never been so committed to art that I would give it priority. In my view, art can inform life only to the extent that our experiences as limited and mortal sentient beings can first inform it—even though the act of creating an artifact like an essay or a book can, and should, surprise its author with new insights.

In recent years, I have been subscribing to the *American Scholar,* for in no other magazine have I so consistently found essays of the sort I'm drawn to. It was the only periodical I knew of that might be interested in the kind of reflective essay I had just written, so I submitted it there. It must have lingered as a doubtful item on somebody's desk before it came to the attention of the editor, who happened to be familiar with my earlier work. She accepted it at once, phoning me to apologize for the delay and telling me how much she had liked it. "Happy Trails to All" appeared soon after—in the autumn 2001 issue—and later was chosen by the editorial board as the best essay to appear in the magazine that year.

It's embarrassing for a veteran writer like me—one who has always considered his writing to be above all else a spiritual activity—to admit that such a crass element as ego has anything to do with his creativity. In filching the title—*Why I Write*—of one of her essays from George Orwell, Joan Didion says the reason for writing is obvious from the sound of the pronoun "I" in all three of those words. Her remark is more than clever: after all, one writes for an audience and is imposing (particularly in an essay) his or her views on other people. Even a writer whose wish is to subsume the "I" into something larger— call it humanity, the natural world, or the universe—can't dismiss the centrality of the self to such a desire.

In any event, the response first by the *American Scholar's* editor and then by her editorial board stimulated me to continue writing. This magazine published another essay, and other periodicals did as well. For book publication, those authors whose motivations for writing—whatever their age—are related to mine will doubtless have to depend on independent presses run by publishers and editors similar to the late Bill Whitehead, who as editor-in-chief at Dutton called me into his office to explain the quandary he faced. Fortunately for me, an independent publisher found my work appealing enough not only to reprint a book of mine in 2000—that edition of *To a Distant Island,* an account of Chekhov's journey to a prison colony off the coast of Siberia, is more handsome than the original one—but to ask me some months ago to submit a manuscript of my uncollected work, a substantial portion of which was written after the publication of "Happy Trails to All." That request resulted in the present book.

This brief essay is intended as a note of gratitude to all who over the decades have abetted the ego that I find such an irritant, yet a necessity for my writing. They include readers who have come across my work and have written me, as well as former editors like Bill Whitehead (whose name is representative of many), and present ones like Anne Fadiman of the *American Scholar* and others. My appreciation is also to those staff members whose editorial work includes a painstaking concern, in the pursuit of clarity, for syntax and punctuation. Such attention reminds me of a lecture the late Josephine Miles—a poet and scholar of inestimable influence on a number of writers as well as many others who studied under her—gave at Cornell at least a quarter of a century ago. The increasing severity of a disease contracted in childhood had cost her the use of her legs. So that the auditors wouldn't be distracted from what she had to say, she had asked to be carried to a chair behind a desk long before her audience arrived. Her subject was the proper use of adjectives and punctuation marks, matters she made so captivating and important that her audience listened intently to her every word. That lecture was such an affirmative one—to humanity, and to all the possibilities that lie before us, those glittering hopes of a better world—that it made me happy in a way no other scholarly lecture ever has.

For me, good editing is an affirmation like that: testimony that one's words are worthy of close attention.

Acknowledgments

"The Telescope in the Parlor" first appeared in the *American Poetry Review,* November–December 2004.

"Idyll" first appeared in *The Book of Love,* edited by Diane Ackerman and Jeanne Mackin, W.W. Norton & Co., 1998.

"Happy Trails to All" first appeared in the *American Scholar,* Vol. 70, No. 4, Autumn 2001.

"On Being Human" first appeared in the *American Scholar,* Vol. 72, No. 1, Winter 2003.

"Two Anonymous Writers: E. M. Forster and Anton Chekhov" first appeared in *E. M. Forster: A Human Exploration,* edited by G. K. Das and John Beer, New York University Press, 1979.

"A Faded Portrait" first appeared in *Pequod,* issue 34, 1992.

"The Moral Backbone of *The Anatomy of Memory*" first appeared in *Andre Dubus: Tributes,* edited by Donald Anderson, Xavier University Press, 2001.

"Reality and Imagination in Literature and Psychology" first appeared in the *Bookpress,* December 1999, under the title "On the Tip of the Tongue."

"Ubiquitous Augustine" first appeared in the *Bookpress,* May 2000, under the title "Meaning and Metaphor."

"Rereading Ammons's Long Poems" first appeared in the *American Poetry Review,* May-June 2003.

"The River Runs Through Us" first appeared in the *Bookpress,* November 2003.

"Some Views about Cuba for the Delegation That Couldn't Visit" first appeared in *Epoch,* Vol. 51, No. 1, 2002.

"Nurture for the Damn Ego" first appeared in the *American Scholar,* Vol. 73, No. 4, Autumn 2004.